"MR. KING,

YOU'RE HAVING A
HEART ATTACK"

"MR. KING, YOU'RE HAVING A HEART ATTACK"

How a Heart Attack and
Bypass Surgery Changed My Life

BY LARRY KING
WITH B.D. COLEN

With an Introduction by
C. Everett Koop, M.D., Surgeon General

**Delacorte
Press**

Published by
Delacorte Press
Bantam Doubleday Dell Publishing Group, Inc.
666 Fifth Avenue
New York, New York 10103

Dr. C. Everett Koop wrote the Introduction to this book in his
official capacity as Surgeon General to warn of the dangers of
smoking. He did not receive any compensation for the
Introduction, and the Introduction is in the public domain.

Library of Congress Cataloging in Publication Data

King, Larry, 1933—
    Mr. King, you're having a heart attack: how a heart attack
and bypass surgery changed my life / by Larry King with B. D.
Colen; with an introduction by C. Everett Koop.
        p.   cm.
    ISBN 0-440-50039-7
    1. King, Larry, 1933-   —Health.   2. Heart—Infarction
—Patients—United States—Biography.   3. Aortocoronary
bypass—Patients—United States—Biography.   I. Colen, B. D.
II. Title.   III. Title: Mister King, you're having a heart attack.
RC685.I6K476 1989
362.1'961'237'00—dc19
[B]   88-23558
                                                           CIP

Manufactured in the United States of America

February 1989

10 9 8 7 6 5 4 3 2 1

BG

To the memory of my mother, Jennie Zeiger, whose husband died of this disease much too early. And to my dear brother, Martin Zeiger, for whom I wish only what he wishes for himself.

Acknowledgments

I would like to thank Dr. Edward Brown for reading the manuscript for technical accuracy. B. D. Colen, who in addition to being a coauthor on this venture became a lifelong friend. Bob Woolf, who is more than just a representative: he is a true friend and confidant; he and his wife, Ann, provided great comfort to me in a time of need. As always, Herb and Ellen Cohen, who are there for me, as was my dear sister-in-law, Ellen David.

Thanks are due as well to our literary agent, Jay Acton, who conceived of this project and was there with help and advice at all times.

And to Chaia, Andy, and Dori: thank you for always being there.

Contents

Contents

Introduction

It is fair to say that America is preoccupied with health. A glance at the headlines of any paper—to say nothing of the weekly or monthly health supplements—gives strong support to that observation. Many books on health have been authored and for some of those books I have been asked to write an introduction. Such requests are very legitimate and my basic instinct is to say yes. However, it is not considered the best protocol for the Surgeon General to write a preface for a book, and in addition, if I were to do it as often as asked, my words would cease to mean very much.

I am writing the Introduction for this book for several reasons. I was with the author the night he had his heart attack; the proceeds of this book will go to charity; but most important, this book has a message: It can save lives, and that is what my mission is all about.

Larry King's story has a happy ending. He is with us and he is as active as ever in bringing information and enjoyment to thousands of people. His story is important for others to read because he is honest. The story of his denial of the underlying heart disease he knew he had and of the angina he was experiencing is typical but not often talked about by laymen.

Many people have recovered from heart attacks, but few of them are frank about the fear that pervades the lives of post-heart attack victims. Larry tells of that part of his history convincingly, as he does the whole sequence from heart attack through angioplasty, back to work, the return of symptoms, facing surgery, the procedure itself, and living because of surgery.

Larry King's story has such a happy ending because the human mind and body are marvelously resilient. But you can quickly run out of miracles as you make your way in the dynamic and complex world such as the one in which Larry King lived.

I would like to focus on what I think is Larry King's greatest risk factor—smoking. If the author didn't expect an antismoking message, he didn't think carefully about one of the risks you take when you ask the Surgeon General to write the Introduction for your book.

In the mass of information on smoking and health I have tried to put before the American people during my tenure as Surgeon General, I started first with cancer, which is the best-known sequel to long exposure to cigarette smoke. My next report was on cardiovascular disease and documented in a scientific way much of what this book tells in a readable and believable style. Then I focused on chronic obstructive lung disease such as emphysema and bronchitis. After that came the cumulative effects of smoking and other environmental hazards at the work site.

In 1986 the *Surgeon General's Report on Smoking and Health* found passive or side-stream smoking to be productive of disease. One of those diseases was cancer of the lung. The report further indicated that mere separation in the same room of smokers and non-smokers is not protective. All these reports were leading up to the one presented in May of 1988, which demonstrated, on the basis of over 2,000 scientific papers, that tobacco is addicting, that nicotine is the substance in tobacco that causes the addiction, and that the addiction to nicotine is by the same process as is the addiction to cocaine and heroin.

Larry King knew all about the dangers of cigarette smoking. The night he had his heart attack we discussed it on his program *Live with Larry King.* In spite of all the things that we knew, he baffled his colleagues by continuing to smoke. Why? He was addicted to nicotine.

Like 43 million other Americans, Larry King has quit smoking. As he was lying in a hospital emergency room thinking he might be facing death, he made a promise to himself that was self-rewarding: "If I live, I'll never smoke again." Fortunately, he hasn't.

One benefit of my report to Congress and the American people on nicotine as an addictive substance is that smokers are now free of the delusion that they have a dirty habit that they can quit as soon as circumstances are right and they make the decision to do so. Now they know that they have a real problem and one need not be ashamed of seeking professional help to correct addiction.

An interesting spin-off has been that the friends, spouses, parents, and children of smokers, now knowing that tobacco is addictive, are sympathetic rather than castigating or derisive.

I would have been disappointed if the tobacco industry had had a reasonable response to the report on addiction, but they didn't fail me. Said their spokesman, "The claims that smokers are addicts defy common sense and contradict the fact that people quit smoking every day." A senator from a tobacco-growing state thought I had mistaken the enemy.

Our enemy—tobacco—kills in excess of 300,000 people a year. Contrast this with 125,000 who die each year from alcohol and about 8,000 who die of overdoses of drugs or a combination of drugs and alcohol and you can see what the real enemy is.

Without knowing it, Larry King was a marvelous example of the seductive addiction of tobacco. When he needed to be alert and put forth an extra effort, he smoked in a way that produced the desired result. When the stress was gone and he wanted to relax, he smoked in a different way, set up a different set of physiologic responses in his body, and was able to get the relaxation he sorely desired and needed.

Most of the people who read this book will have an interest in heart attacks. A great many of them will be smokers. The message—stop smoking—is vital to their survival.

We've known for years that the best success in any antismoking effort is in one-on-one encouragement that smokers get from family members and close friends, but especially from their physicians.

In this book Larry King could become your best friend and his advice could save your life. Heed it.

C. Everett Koop, M.D., Sc.D.
Surgeon General
U.S. Public Health Service

"MR.KING,
YOU'RE HAVING A
HEART ATTACK"

1

February 24, 1987:
Heart Attack!

FOUR A.M., FEBRUARY 24, 1987. THE END OF A LONG day, a medical day for me. The guests on my CNN television show seven hours earlier had been Frank Young, the commissioner of the federal Food and Drug Administration, and U.S. Surgeon General C. Everett Koop. The hour of television had gone well, but Koop's last words to me as he left the studio were prophetic:

"Boy, you oughta stop smoking."

I smoked all the time: shaving, in the shower, in bed, during meals, during commercials in my show. Even with Koop there. I didn't think anything of his warning as I drove from the CNN studios in downtown Washington to the Mutual Radio Network studios across the Potomac in Crystal City. I was looking forward to my 11 P.M. to 4 A.M. radio show. My guest for that show was David Halberstam, who's always a wonderful interview. A girlfriend of mine, visiting from Phoenix, was at the radio show with me and I was going to spend the night with her at her hotel. At the end of the show David left. I did the open phones, and then I drove back through the deserted, snow-covered streets to Washington to my friend's hotel.

But something was wrong. When I got there, at about 4:30, I told her that I was feeling "sluggish," the only way I could explain it, and said I was going home to bed —to get some sleep. On the way home I started getting this pain across my shoulder. Right shoulder down the right arm. I'd had what you'd call discomfort when I left the studio, but this was more than discomfort. I wasn't feeling right. You know how something's wrong but you don't know what it is?

Before I go any further, I have an admission to make: When it came to my health, I was one of the world's great deniers. I knew my symptoms weren't typical heart attack symptoms. But here I was, a fifty-three-year-old, twenty-pounds overweight, cholesterol-consuming, three-pack-a-day smoker whose father died of heart disease at forty-four, and I couldn't figure out what was happening to me? On top of which, I *knew* that I had coronary artery disease.

I had first become aware of my heart problems six years earlier, in March 1981. I was walking on Fifth Avenue in New York City, walking in my jaunty, brisk way. I was doing a radio show for a week in New York. I had just come from Nat Sherman's, tobacconist. I loved his cigarettes. They were a wonderful cigarette. Great flavor—and they were expensive and I liked to spoil myself by buying them. Well, I was walking back from Nat Sherman's to the Hilton Hotel, and suddenly I got this unusual pain in my chest that I'd never felt before. Had no idea what it was. I stopped walking, it went away immediately. I started to walk, it started again. It felt like I had just run a mile. It felt like your heart feels when you've run up and down the stairs. All I was doing was walking. It was weird. So I didn't know what to make of it. I got back to the hotel, I sat down, I had no other pain. I sat down on the bed, no pain. That night I went and did the radio show fine. The next day was windy. I'm walking along, the same thing happens. The shortness of breath, catching my breath. Stops as soon as I stopped walking.

When I got back to Washington I didn't know what to do about this new problem. I told my radio producer about it and she said, "You haven't had a checkup in a while, why don't you go over and get one?" Pretty obvious thing to do when you're having chest pain. But there was the denial. Well, I went to Georgetown University Medical Center and they gave me one of those top-to-toe checkups—including a complete cardiac workup with a stress test. As soon as it was over the doctor said to me, "Mr. King, you have a heart problem."

I didn't know any cardiologists I could think of, so I did what you do when you need the name of a doctor: I called my best friend, Herb Cohen, in Chicago. He told me to send the report from Georgetown to his nephew, Dr. David Blumenthal, a staff cardiologist at New York Hospital-Cornell University Medical Center. (There's the denial again: I'm thinking I don't know any cardiologists and I've known David since he was five years old.) So I had everything sent to David, who calls and says, "Larry, you have coronary artery disease. You oughta stop smoking and you oughta watch yourself and there's a cardiologist I went to school with I'll recommend. He's in Baltimore. Is that too far for you?" I said, "No." And I went to see him and became his patient. And about six months later he decided I really needed a catheterization—an angiogram—if he was gonna know what was going on with my heart. That's the test where they make an incision in an artery in your thigh, snake a very thin tube—a catheter— through the artery all the way to your heart, and then inject radioactive dye and film it as it goes through the coronary arteries. Shows them just where the blockages are, and how bad they are. They don't like to do the cath unless they think you really need it, because it does involve some minor risk. But he decided I needed it, so he ordered it at Johns Hopkins. That was the first time I had checked into a hospital since I had a mastoidec- tomy when I was three years old.

After the catheterization the doctor came in to see me and said, "Well, it's fifty-fifty. We can do a bypass, you've got one artery completely blocked off. We don't know when that happened, it could have been years ago. You've got another one in trouble, another one is pretty good. Can you change your life-style? If we treated you aggressively with drugs, do you think you could try to stop smoking, change what you eat?"

"Naturally," I said—as an alternative to having my chest sawed in half—"the answer is yes." But I never could stop smoking. And while I changed some diet patterns, I never really changed much. It might have made a difference if I had, but given the blockages I already had, the disease might have caught up with me sooner or later anyway—although it is possible that if I'd really taken the early warning seriously, I might have managed with just medication and no surgery. But we'll never know now. Anyway, I went for check- ups every six months. I got stress tests. I did okay. Some better than others. I never had what you'd call a positive stress test. I never had one where the doctor said, "Let's get him into surgery." I brought my weight down some. He said, "You ought to stop smoking." He was never aggressive with me. He'd say, "You ought to think about not smoking." Of course I now realize it was up to me, not the doctor, to be aggressive about changing my life-style.

In the intervening years I had occasional chest pain, but I'd just pop a Nitrostat—a nitroglycerin tablet. Oh, if I had it once every three months, it was a lot. Then in December of 1986 and January of 1987, I had been doing a lot of speaking around the country and my career was rolling, I had the CNN show and my schedule was pretty packed. Even through the denial I realized that I was getting more shortness of breath at airports and stuff.

So here it is, the early morning of February 24, and I'm feeling funny. My daughter, Chaia, who is living with me, is asleep. She was nineteen then, a student at American University. She didn't have classes on the twenty-fourth. So I didn't have to worry about waking her up when I got to the apartment, but for some reason I didn't wake her. I guess I didn't want her to worry. But as soon as I got home it started—this damn aching pain. It would come and go. And I went to sleep. I never thought of taking a nitroglycerin for it. It wasn't a chest pain. I wasn't short of breath. I wasn't sweating. There was nothing classically "heart attack" about this. It was a right shoulder pain going down the right arm slightly. I woke up around 6:30 A.M. because it was getting worse. I had a decision to make: Do I call my regular doctor or do I call my cardiologist? I thought to myself,

"Well, let's take the cardiologist first so that I know this isn't my heart." So I called my cardiologist in Baltimore and he was just getting up to go make his rounds. He said, "Well, that sure doesn't sound like a heart attack. It's very atypical. Sounds like gallbladder. Take some Maalox."

So I took some Maalox and the pain subsided. I said, "Jesus, he was right." Then, at about 7:15, the pain came back. I called the doctor again. He asked if I could make it to Baltimore to see him. It was a normal thing to ask because we're only talking about the right shoulder here, you know. We're not talking about someone doubled up in chest pain. I said I'd try.

I started to walk up the stairs, just fourteen steps, of my duplex apartment—and then the pain got ferocious. I just couldn't get up those stairs. So I called the doctor back and he told me to drive to George Washington University Medical Center. It's about three minutes from me, right over the bridge. He told me to get them to take a cardiogram and have them call him immediately. He said he'd be waiting at Johns Hopkins.

For some reason I'll never understand, I didn't wake my daughter to ask her to take me to GW. Instead, I called Tammy Haddad, my TV producer. All I said was, "Tammy, I think I gotta go to the hospital." Then I just hung up. There was no "What are your symptoms?" Nothing. I just knew she'd come. She's that kind of person: totally and absolutely dependable. She must have really gunned it, because she lives twenty minutes away but she showed up ten minutes later.

Now it's around 9:30 in the morning, and as soon as we arrive at GW the pain goes away completely. You know the old story: You call the repair man and say,

"Come fix my television." He shows up, it's working perfectly, and you're out seventy-five bucks. Anyway, I had no idea what was happening to me. After all, one time I took the Nitrostat and the pain went away, which sounds like it was the heart. But then the next time I took Maalox and—bingo! No pain. Which sounded like something other than the heart. And I had no pain in the chest. And I had no shortness of breath. I just had no idea what this was. No idea. That's the absolute truth.

So we pulled up in front of the hospital and I said, "Tammy, I'm feeling fine. Wait here. If there's a long line, I'm going back home." As luck would have it, I go inside and immediately they chase her away because she was in that emergency zone where ambulances pull up. So they made her go off and park. Meanwhile, I go inside and there are a lot of people there. A lot of snow-related accidents. I look around and see that in every one of the cubicles, the staff is writing up case histories of people. I see a guy getting his arm bandaged. And I wasn't feeling terrific but I didn't have any pain. I guess I was feeling . . . I don't know how I was feeling. I had no pain. I started to go back out the door.

A guy comes over, works at the hospital. I still don't know what his job is—dressed like a doctor, but not a doctor. Sort of like an orderly. But he had a clipboard. He had some function in the emergency room. He came over to me and he said, "Are you feeling okay?"

I said, "Well, I've had some pain and my doctor told me to come over, but the pain's gone and I'm gonna leave." He said, "Well, you look very pale, very gray. Are you a cardiac patient?" I said, "Yes. It was my cardiologist who told me to come over." Boy, you ever want to get taken care of fast in an emergency room, just say "cardiologist" or "chest pain." The next thing I knew I was in a cubicle. They had my shirt open, had the EKG on me, had an intravenous line, an IV, in my wrist, they had taken blood. No "Let me see your Blue Cross card." No forms. I never filled out an insurance form. I still don't know whether anyone filled that form out, but somebody must have. That's only one of the reasons why GW is a good emergency room. It's where President Reagan and Jim Brady were taken when they were shot. Anyway, they send for a cardiologist. Enter Dr. Warren Levy. Beard. A cardiac fellow, which they tell me means he's already an internist and now doing special training in cardiology. A nice guy.

 Boy, you ever want to get taken care of fast in an emergency room, just say "cardiologist" or "chest pain."

Anyway, he told me that my EKG was okay and said that he'd called my cardiologist in Baltimore to let him know what was going on. I felt a really tremendous relief then, and told him so. Then he burst my newly inflated bubble of denial with a big BUT. . . .

"But I have to tell you, we don't like the way you look. I don't normally work in the emergency room. But I'm down here now, so would you try a little experiment with me?" I asked what he wanted me to do and he asked, "Would you wait for the pain to come back?

Could we give it a half hour? If it doesn't come back, we know. I'll wait if you'll wait." I said, "Okay."

By this time Tammy's parked the car. She comes back inside. I said, "We're waiting for the pain." You know, like it's humorous. Of course there was really nothing funny about it. As Dr. Levy later explained it to me, the emergency room doctors—who weren't cardiologists—were puzzled about what was happening to me because my symptoms were so atypical. So first they called down the cardiology resident from the cardiac care unit, and then he called Levy.

At this point he started medications designed to stop an angina attack—intravenous nitroglycerin and what are called calcium channel blockers. The EKG did have changes, which convinced Levy that I was having a heart attack. I started firing questions at him. I guess they were typical for someone who finds himself in an emergency room: "How can you be sure it's my heart? Some of the other doctors thought it might be my gallbladder. Could it just be gas?" A little bit of denial, but at the same time I was focusing on the realities at hand. "Am I going to be here a long time? My producer's here, what kind of plans do I need to make?" Very appropriate and level-headed, but at the same time very anxious.

Dr. Warren Levy on Heart Attack Pain:

When asked if they're experiencing pain, a lot of patients having heart attacks will say no, because in fact what they're feeling is not a pain in the sense of what you and I think of as a pain. They're feeling discomfort. They're feeling a sensation which they don't describe as pain. You have to be very careful when you're speaking to someone: "Are you feeling pain?" "No." "Are you feeling any sort of discomfort in your chest?" "Yes! It feels like an elephant's sitting on me!" A lot of times patients don't define that as a pain. The classic chest pain or chest discomfort syndrome begins just behind the breastbone as sort of a chest pressure, which can sometimes spread to the left shoulder, down the left arm. Occasionally it's associated with shortness of breath, some cold sweats, nausea, and that kind of thing. Larry's was very different, and his electrocardiogram was virtually normal.

But when I spoke with Larry, took a history, and examined him, I learned that although his symptom complex was atypical, it was *fairly typical for him.*

I sure was anxious! Something was obviously *very* wrong. I was still feeling discomfort that I can't describe. Just general discomfort telling me that something's wrong here. And then, here comes the pain. And now it comes like a thunderbolt! It hits me in the right shoulder, right down the right arm into the right elbow. And it's aching. It's like the ache from a wisdom tooth but in the arm. You had a heart attack, you know what I'm talking about. You never had one, you can't even imagine it. You know how, sometimes when you've eaten much too much, you get a sort of shoulder, arm ache? Well, take the worst indigestion like that you've ever experienced, combine it with the worst toothache you ever had, and then, while that's going on, figure a Mosler safe falls off the roof and hits you on that same shoulder and arm—then you've got an *idea* what I'm talking about. It's pain that makes you sweat, makes your skin go gray. And now they give me another EKG. And check my blood gases—isn't that the greatest medical term you've ever heard?—while the pain is on. And I remember lying in Cubicle 8. The doctor goes out, someone takes the EKG, rips it off the machine, and they run it out to him, Levy. Meanwhile

▶ **"Mr. King, there's only one way to tell you this. You're having a heart attack. And you're having it right this minute. All the rest this morning was a prelude. This is it. The Big Kahuna."**

the blood-gas report—giving him the proportions and amount of oxygen and other gases in the blood—is being brought to him. He has both these things. He has the EKG, and it looks like he's holding it up to the light to read it better. I'm sitting there with this pain. And suddenly he, two nurses, and another doctor all make a U-turn. And they make a beeline right for me. And I swear to God—how can I think of humor at a time like this?—but the thought in my mind was "This ain't gonna be a muscle pull. This *ain't* gonna be a muscle pull!" which made me smile to myself. And Dr. Levy said, "Mr. King, there's only one way to tell you this. You're having a heart attack. And you're having it right this minute. All the rest this morning was a prelude. This is it. The Big Kahuna."

I said to him, "Am I gonna die?"

And I recall Levy saying, "There's three great chances that you're gonna live." And they're working on me now. Everything's happening in double time. Strapping up, things are going in. And I see them bring in this big, big bag of liquid, which I later learned was tPA. Huge. As large a bag as I've ever seen. Like four times larger than the blood-transfusion bags that I've seen since. And they get my arm all hooked up and I got this thing there. He said, "The three reasons are: one, you're having your heart attack in the best place to have it, in the hospital; two, it's a right-side attack. They have a 75 percent survival rate, so if we did nothing, you'd still have three chances out of four of living. We have a third advantage at this hospital. We're one of about twenty-five hospitals in America using the experimental drug tPA. Now I have to read this to you and I have to read it to you real fast, Mr. King. And then I want you to sign this. I know you're gonna sign it because the first thing I'm gonna tell you is we've been using tPA here under the TIMI program for eighteen months and we've had great success."

Dr. Warren Levy on the Testing of tPA

The TIMI—Thrombolysis In acute Myocardial Infarction—trials were designed to test tPA—tissue plasminogen activator, the best of a new group of drugs often called "clot busters." There were certain criteria that had to be met before someone could be entered into the trials.

The drug tPA, which has now been approved for general use but was still investigational when we gave it to Larry, is designed to break up those blood clots that can block off the blood flow in an artery. In order to properly test whether tPA did patients any good, it could be given only to those who were clearly having a heart attack when measured against certain symptoms. When you test a new drug you have to know that patients have the same symptoms, or problems, or you don't have any way to tell what it means when one does well and another doesn't. Larry's atypical symptoms and first EKG didn't meet the TIMI criteria. But when we examined the next EKG, we saw that, fortunately for Larry, he met the minimal criteria for inclusion in the study.

So, while Levy is explaining the tPA testing procedures to me, there's an amazing commotion going on around me. People with tubes, bags, needles, and machines all over the place. Levy explains that the sooner they can get an IV in and start the tPA, the better off I'll be. He gives me a brief explanation of the risks and benefits and then asks, "Do you think you're interested?"

"Yes, by all means, don't waste time," I told him.

Now there are even more people running around me. Levy warned me that a lot's going to be happening now. They're going to be putting in arterial lines, there's going to be a lot of activity around my bed. He told me to just pay attention to what he's telling me. Let him know how I'm feeling, if anything's bothering me, if the pain's getting worse. Just tell him, just listen to him. I think he feels it's easier for a patient to just focus on one person when there's a lot of activity around him. That way, he explained, he could be sure that someone would hear me if I said, "Hey! The pain's getting a lot worse," or, "I'm awfully short of breath."

At this point, while Dr. Levy was reading me the informed consent, I remember the nurse was standing by with the tPA all hooked up. I was still feeling pain, but then Levy yells—and I thought this was really funny, despite the circumstances—he yells, "Give Mr. King some morphine!" I'd never had morphine, in all my life. I'd seen war movies, and in war movies whenever a guy was really in pain on the beach, and they'd say, "Give him morphine!" someone would say, "But, Captain, we're low." "Give it to him," the captain would say. "But we're low on morphine." "Give it to him." And he got it, and it always meant pleasure for whoever got it. If a guy had a right arm shot off, he got the morphine and—"Ah!" So because of my expectation, I had an enormous feeling of pleasure. He's reading me this thing and they shoot me with morphine. And I ask, "Why is the pain still here?"

Then Levy's explaining to me, "Mr. King, when you're having a heart attack, and the blood can't get through, there's no such thing as a painkiller." So he says, "Sign." I scrawled "Larry King." As I finished the "g"—pfft—the nurse put it in. It was not five minutes before the pain went away completely. And it went like *that! Like that!* The clot was broken. The whole hospital stay. No more pain, no more discomfort, no more nothing. The pain was gone.

You know, the strangest thing about that first night in the cardiac care unit was that it scared the hell out of the people who came to see me, but it didn't bother me a bit. The doctors tell me that a fair number of patients suffer from something called CCU, or ICU, psychosis—they have serious difficulty dealing with being surrounded by all those tubes, wires, machines . . . to say nothing of sick people. But I didn't have any of it. Piece of cake. And you know why? No pain. I didn't have a drop of pain. That pain was so bad that when they took that pain away, I mean . . . it was just such an incredible relief. And when you think about it, it was the first time in months that I was truly free of all pain, discomfort, whatever. Even though Levy told me the next twenty-four hours were very critical. He said, "Obviously we've stopped the spread, now we don't know the damage. And we won't know until tomorrow and we're not going to bother with looking to see what it is to-night. We're gonna let you get some rest." They drugged me up and I slept most of that night with the tPA. I had survived the first crucial twenty-four hours after a heart attack.

2
Angioplasty

AS I LOOK BACK ON THAT FIRST DAY AND EVENING, I realize now that it must have been almost as hard on my daughter, Chaia, and my friends as it was on me. Think about it: The person having the heart attack just has to lie there and live through it; everyone around the person has to deal with what's going on. And that ain't easy.

Chaia has told me that she wasn't really struck by the fact of my mortality until she saw me in the cardiac care unit. "The first time I saw him in the emergency room was certainly emotional. I mean, I cried. But I think I was just really upset because something frightening had happened. But I wasn't struck yet by the fact that someone close to you can die because I had only faced one death in the family and that was a great-grandmother. But while he was in cardiac care, when all the machines were in there and he looked awful and people were coming in and I had to call people and tell them what happened—then it was like my life turned over in a matter of hours. That's when I realized that he could die."

I think that what Chaia was going through at that point was typical for a kid of any age who first comes face-to-face with a parent's mortality. She'd known for years that I had heart trouble, but she'd protected herself the way we all do: She hadn't been able to, or wanted to, connect the idea of a "heart condition" with the reality that I might die. On some level I'm sure she thought I'd live forever. Hell, that's what I thought!

I think that the other person who was most affected by my heart attack was Herbie Cohen, my best friend in the world. Herbie—who I played with as a kid in Brooklyn and still play with—arrived from Chicago. As Herbie recalls it, he didn't even stop at the reception desk at the hospital when he got there on the evening of the twenty-fourth. Herbie says he "didn't stop at the desk because I know if I stop at the desk, I don't get to see Larry. I mean, I'm familiar with hospitals: 'Oh no, sir, we have regulations here, and no, you can't see this person.' I knew that he was in intensive care or something, special cardiac care, and I figured Chaia was there so I wanted to go up there to find out exactly how he was. And then I looked on the wall map to see where cardiac care was, whatever floor it was on. I remember going past the desk, you know, walking like I was part of the hospital surroundings, very official person, knew where I was going and went on the elevator, got out at the right floor, then looked for cardiac care, walked through the door, and saw Chaia."

Chaia was still real upset when Herbie showed up, but she wasn't so distraught that she didn't see what happened when Herbie saw me lying there in the cardiac care unit for the first time. "I saw in Herbie's eyes the fact that they had been friends so long and had been

children together," says Chaia. "Both their lives were
flashing before their eyes. Because if Dad had died, a
part of Herbie would have died and that past would
have died, so I saw them both realizing the importance
of the past and how scary this event was. Herbie was
scared." I think that what happened was Herbie and I
looked into each other's eyes and instantly aged about
forty years. You see, up till then, we hadn't aged in each
other's eyes. We were still kids of twelve in Bensonhurst. But at that moment Herbie saw the truth in
my eyes, and I saw it reflected back: "We're all grown
up. In fact, we're in our fifties. This ain't kid stuff anymore. Our lives are more than half over. It's pretty
scary stuff.

 **"We're all grown up. In fact,
we're in our fifties. This ain't
kid stuff anymore. Our lives
are more than half over. It's
pretty scary stuff."**

"So I'm in the CCU with my best friend from child-
hood, and there he was lying on this bed with all sorts of
machines there, you know, mostly like you see in the
movies or *Ben Casey*—which dates me. You know, these
things went *bur-r-r-r!* and he's wired up and he's got
tubes running in and out of him and he's being fed
intravenously and he looks very pale. He looks really
pale, I mean, there's no color in his face at all. Very,
very pale. Like, when I was a kid, we used to take

someone's hand and squeeze it, we used to squeeze the blood out of it, we used to call it giving someone a 'dead hand.' And that's the way his face looked. But he feels better and he's telling me the story, and as I'm talking to him, he moves suddenly, he turns, and the monitor that's going toward his heart or his brain, it suddenly runs flat. You know what I'm thinking: 'My God! The guy's dying!' . . . You know, he pulled out a plug 'cause he turned. You know, I moved, he turned, he pulled out a plug, and then I say, 'Oh! Get the nurse! Press a button or something!' "

I know that seeing me lying there was not easy for Herbie. It's hard to explain how close we are. We were both eight when we met. And the interesting thing about us is, we haven't changed that much. Herbie likes to tell the story about how one night, during a period when we hadn't seen each other in a few years because we were both so busy with our careers, he was lying in bed with his wife one night and she turned to him and asked, "Do you love me the most of anyone in the whole world?" As Herbie tells it, he said, " 'Well, I really love you a lot, I would say you're number four.' I thought that, you know, it was like a joke—of course I loved her the most. But she said, 'What do you mean, I'm number four, who's one?' Well, I said, 'I like Larry the most . . . Larry's number one; Whohah's number two,' you know. 'So and So's number three. But you're four and that's good, 'cause you didn't start out that high.' She didn't laugh. Didn't think it was funny," Herbie says, laughing. "Larry would. That's how we are."

When I was lying there Herbie had a sense of my vulnerability—and I knew that he did too. I think we were both silently reviewing all those years together, all the laughs, all the gags. And the sense of immortality we'd had, we never thought about really taking care of ourselves. Somehow, Herbie and I both *knew* that nothing bad was gonna happen to *us.* Neither of us took care of ourselves at all. For instance, we would go out to eat and we would have steak, of course, what else? Home-fried potatoes, we liked that quite a bit. The only thing we ate that was ever healthy was we had chopped salad. We would call it Gerber's Child Salad, like babies, you know, we would chop it. But we would put Roquefort dressing on it or something. We'd eat the bread, the butter. I guess you could say neither of us had a life-style that was concerned with health. I smoked. He smoked. Herbie smoked cigars—ten, fifteen a day, inhaled them.

But we didn't talk about any of that that night. All I remember was that we laughed a lot. Herbie and I always find something to laugh about. I guess when we get together we're still just a couple of silly twelve-year-olds. Even after a heart attack.

The next day was an interesting one. Informative. And, thank God, less dramatic than the day before. The first thing was they had to explain the second part of the tPA study to me. By now Levy's boss, Dr. Richard Katz, was involved. He became my cardiologist in Washington. Anyway, he explained to me that it was standard operating procedure to come back to the patient twenty-four hours later, before anything else is done to the patient in the study, to ask him to re-sign the consent form when things are a bit calmer than they were initially.

Patients didn't have to stay in the study at that point. At least they've been able to give you tPA by then. You know, it's interesting: Katz says that at one point they tried interviewing patients on what they remembered about signing the consent form the first time. I've forgotten the exact number, but he said something like seventy or so of the patients didn't even remember signing the consent form. And they go through all these efforts—it takes weeks to write consent forms up, show them to the lawyers and hospital review committees, and they pass on it, NIH passes on it, and you've got this ludicrous document. It's not ludicrous, but the setting makes the whole thing impossible. So he says coming back a second time is what makes it much more reasonable and a good idea, whoever's part it was to set it up that way. I had a really typical reaction when the consent form was first read to me: "Why are we wasting time? Shove it in and get going." I'd heard about the drug and this kind of heart attack therapy. It has a lot of simple commonsense appeal about it. I couldn't figure out why they were messing around with having me sign all these forms. "Just give me the drug and save my life!"

When they first offered me a chance to be included in the TIMI study and get tPA, Levy and Katz explained to me that on a random basis half the people in the study are chosen to undergo what they call PCTA— percutaneous transluminal angioplasty, the balloon procedure, balloon angioplasty, after they get the tPA. This means they make an incision in an artery in your leg, take a catheter with a tiny balloon attached, thread it into your leg, up to the heart, into the coronary artery with the blockage, and then inflate the balloon in an

I couldn't figure out why
they were messing around
with having me sign all
these forms. "Just give me the
drug and save my life!"

attempt to at least partially clear away the blockage.
Well, it turned out I had drawn the short straw—so they
wanted to do an angiogram and then the angioplasty.

"Larry had a comfortable, uneventful first night,"
Warren Levy recalls. "His electrocardiograms evolved
in a pattern which was consistent with the type of heart
attack he had had. He remained symptom-free until
the next morning, before he went down for his angioplasty, which was the first time that he was allowed to
get out of bed. And in just the small amount of activity
that involves moving from a bed to a chair and around
the room, he again had some discomfort. He didn't
want to tell anybody about it. But it's not surprising. He
had a very tight blockage in the artery that gave him
the heart attack. Enough blood could get down to the
heart when he was just resting quietly, but even a small
amount of activity would increase the work of the heart
and surpass the supply of blood and oxygen that could
go past that blockage. So on that second hospital day he
went down to the catheterization lab and had angioplasty. Then we confirmed that his coronary artery
disease was not limited only to the artery that had given
him the heart attack."

I really didn't feel any concern as they took me down
for the angioplasty. In the first place, I'd had an angi-

ogram years before at Johns Hopkins, so I had an idea what it would be like. Even more important, I was totally relieved that the pain of the heart attack was gone: I felt like I beat the game. I'd read enough about the early success they had in the trials of tPA—which has since been approved by the FDA—to have faith that it would do the trick. I *knew* the angina was still there, but that didn't surprise me, or even worry me that much. I could deny that it really meant anything. And besides, I figured they were gonna fix me up with the angioplasty. Just so I avoided surgery. First thing I'd said to Levy and Katz was "No surgery!" I did not want my chest cut open. Period. Besides, at that point, being a heavy smoker, I wasn't a good candidate for surgery. So they decided to take the shot with angioplasty. And

 First thing I'd said to Levy and Katz was "No surgery!" I did not want my chest cut open. Period.

they know they only have one shot with the angioplasty. They don't have any more right away because it can increase the chance of a heart attack. If they do it again, it can lead to a break in the artery.

You know, the hardest part of the whole thing was urinating. See, the angiogram is no problem because it only takes about an hour. But the angioplasty takes three hours. And they keep giving you the dye. And then you're forced to urinate and you're lying straight down. And it was impossible to urinate. Anyway, they showed me the blockages on the TV monitor. It was weird seeing my own heart up there, but again, you gotta understand, I'm in a very good frame of mind because I'm out of pain. That's how bad that pain had been.

They said you could see where I had one artery completely blocked off. "Capillaries have taken over," they told me, "that could have been when you were twelve years old." It's one of the wonders of science they don't understand. But the body does some of its own bypassing. You have a blocked artery, sometimes smaller blood vessels carry some blood around the blockage. So I have a bypass going around the main blockage. Not enough, of course. Anyway, Katz said, "What we're gonna do here is take in this balloon, deflated. And you see all these little particles? We're gonna put this balloon in and we're gonna inflate it, and the theory is, we're gonna push the particles up against the artery and we're gonna deflate it and pull it out and hope that the pressure of flow of your blood will keep the artery open like a pipe." I don't remember them asking, "Do you want to do it?" Although they must have. All I remember them saying is, "Here's what we're gonna do." I don't remember if I signed anything. But I must have.

So I watched the whole thing. And the only thing that bothered me was, I got so I couldn't pee. God, I couldn't pee. But it was fascinating to see that thing go in. You know, I'd see all the plaque, looking at it . . . I didn't even know it was me. You didn't look at it as you. It was just interesting. First of all, it's very boring because the lining in your mouth gets very dry and you're just lying there. So the only thing to do is watch. And then when they inflate the balloon, you see the principle work, you see this thing go into the artery. And you see the particles of plaque there. Then they inflate the balloon. And then the catheter comes out. It comes out and then you don't see the particles anymore. So I felt totally cured. That whole process took about three or four hours. You know, they told me that I started with about a 90 percent blockage in the artery that caused the heart attack and I ended up with about 40 percent blockage. Or, looking at the glass as half full, I went from having a 10 percent functioning artery to having one that was 60 percent functioning. And they said that was a success.

For the remaining six days of my hospital stay all I remember is visitors, flowers, and phone calls. We had a list drawn up for security of the people who were allowed to get in to see me. That helped, but it also caused some problems. I remember that one afternoon my old friend Duke Zeibert came by and brought me—of all things—a cheesecake from his restaurant. Went to the front desk and said, "I'm here to see Larry King. I want to drop this off for him." They check the list. He's not on it. They say hit the road. I hear about it later and hit the roof. (I think the way Warren Levy put it was that I "decompensated.") But you can't plan for everything.

As Herbie discovered. After he saw me and convinced himself I was okay, Herbie and his wife, Ellen, flew down to Puerto Rico, where he was supposed to be giving some seminars. Herbie was supposed to stay there working for about five days, but instead he spent most of his time fielding calls about my health from people like Governor Mario Cuomo, Louis Lefkowitz, etc. So he decided it would make a lot more sense to fly back to D.C. and deal with me in person.

"You know," Herbie said, "trying to be Larry's major-domo was not always easy. I mean, face it . . . Larry's a little crazy. For example, he's getting flowers. And Larry, as secure and wonderful as he is, he's insecure. You know, it's constantly, 'Am I getting messages?' This is a guy recovering from a heart attack. 'Are people calling me? Did so-and-so call?' So, anyway, Chaia's got a list of these things and they keep coming to Chaia. And the flowers just keep coming and coming. So I got back there and said, 'He doesn't need all these flowers. We're giving away Larry's flowers.' Chaia liked the idea. So Chaia and I went and we gave away I don't know how many flowers. His room was like a botanical garden. We gave away his flowers, his candy. We asked the nurses if there were people in the hospital who didn't have flowers and the nurses liked the idea of giving them away, so Chaia and I sent the flowers around to the people who didn't have them."

It was pretty amazing. I'm lying there in the hospital wondering why, all of a sudden, nobody's sending any flowers. I mean, one minute I'm in a greenhouse, the next minute—nothin'. And Herbie and Chaia are laughing like hell! I even asked them, "What about the flowers? Aren't I getting any flowers? How come they stopped?" And they tell me they don't have any idea. Of course they were right. As Herbie said to me later, "How many flowers can any one person enjoy?" And the flowers cheered up a lot of people who otherwise wouldn't have gotten any. I didn't know what they'd done with the flowers—I just knew they'd stopped. But at least they didn't stop them before I got these incredible orchids from Raymond Burr. I mean I heard from *everybody.* Even Sinatra. Sinatra sent one of those cards that had to make you feel good. He sent I guess a $200 floral display. And the card said, "Anything you need, Frank." It was amazing. And everybody said the same thing: "Hang in there. You'll make it." 'Cause when you think about it, "heart attack" means *death* to most people. But not to Martin Sheen.

Sheen came to see me late one night, about the fourth or fifth day in the hospital. Mitch Snyder, the activist for the homeless in D.C., came with him. Anyway, I had interviewed Sheen on the show, and we'd become friendly. So when he heard I was in the hospital with a heart attack, he came by and described his heart attack. How he survived it. He had had a heart attack in the Philippines when he was filming *Apocalypse Now,* and they said last rites. But he still smoked; I couldn't believe it. All that and he still smokes now. And I said, "Why do you smoke?" And he says, "Cigarettes are my friends. I like them." But even though I was determined I was never smoking again, he was very comforting to me. He gave me a little piece of crystal that had been given to him when he was having his heart attack. A good-luck piece. And he passed it on to me. And he held my hand. He and Mitch must have stayed three, four hours.

Believe it or not, with the pain gone, and the heart attack and angioplasty behind me, the remaining six days of my eight-day hospitalization were a combination of rest cure and jail time. I was ready to leave whenever Katz and Levy would let me go. On my last day they gave me a stress test—where they have you

exercise and they do an EKG—which they tell me is
standard operating procedure.

Dr. Richard Katz on the Prerelease Stress Test

We gave Larry a mild exercise test,
which is a screening test to make sure
that there's no easily inducible angina.
We test for discomfort or any heartbeat
irregularities on the exercise test. There
were a couple of things that we noted
with that. That exercise test was one
where we combined the exercise
electrocardiogram with a nuclear picture
of the heart and its contraction. What we
do there is inject a radioactive tracer into
the blood as it goes through the heart
and we're able to follow its path. The
patient is lying on a table with his feet
up on a bicyclelike device that's above
the table. You take this image of the
heart pumping while the patient is
exercising and while he's at rest. The
images looked excellent. Larry did not
have any chest pain, no angina. It almost
looked like a missed heart attack or an
aborted heart attack. I thought that
things were very perfect and he was on a
high. He was still on some medication
and we thought about getting much
more serious about his prevention
approaches to further coronary heart
disease. And he had immediately stopped
smoking, which is the single most
important thing a patient can do.

But I now know that Katz was worried, despite the fact that things looked so good. He's told me since that, if I had been his patient longer and he had known me better, he would have started to talk seriously then and there about bypass surgery.

"At that point in time," Katz says now, "I would have preferred to recommend that Larry undergo elective bypass surgery. However, I talked to Larry and I talked to his original cardiologist. I purposely did not say to Larry, 'Okay, this is it, you must have bypass now,' though it would have been my preference to do so. For years he had been very anxious about the possibility of having to have bypass surgery, even though it had been recommended to him previously. And the coronary artery disease he had now was only worse, not better, than on previous catheterizations. But at this point I wanted him to get over this, get a little bit away from the heart attack and see that he could go on and be himself for a while before really approaching that issue. Since I had not been his doctor before, I did not have the kind of relationship with him where I felt I could barge in and confront him on this obviously sensitive issue. I couldn't say, 'I've known you for forty-eight hours—put your life on the line and have heart surgery.' I base my decision on whether to pursue the subject on the patient's level of anxiety. I sometimes wait. As long as the patient is stable, there's no rush. But I certainly knew he was going to need it. In fact, over the months to come, I was looking for the first excuse so that I could convince him in a rational way. Some patients really have to be hurting, that is, they have to have major symptoms to want to face the risks of having surgery. Here he was soon after a heart attack without

having any angina chest pain or, in his case, right shoulder pain. I had to wait."

I wanted to get back to work as soon as I could. So
when they checked me out of the hospital, my denial
took over again. I was off to Florida for a much-needed
rest. I was home free with this heart disease nonsense
behind me. After all, I'd beaten the Big Kahuna. Or so I
thought.

3
Fear and Depression

BY THE BEGINNING OF MARCH I'M OUT OF THE HOSPI-
tal and on my way to Miami for a couple of weeks. I
wanted to see the Orioles in spring training. I took a
commercial flight down and this funny thing happened. I found myself sitting in first class with Alexan-
der Haig and Eugene McCarthy. Just the three of us.
Before the plane takes off this guy boards, walks
through first class, and sees the three of us sitting there
alone. He shakes his head and says, "Shit! If this plane
goes down, *my* name doesn't make the papers." I don't
know who he was, but it was a great line. Anyway, on
the way down, Haig and I talked about his bypass surgery. I remember him saying to me, "You might need a
bypass someday, but don't worry. It's a piece of cake."
But I didn't want to think about surgery or heart disease. Or my heart attack. I'm not feeling any pain and I
just want to get down to Florida, get a tan, see some ball
games. Which is exactly what I did.

But as I was doing all this something started to un-
nerve me. It should have been a calm, relaxing time.
But it wasn't. While I was in Florida the fear started. I'd

lived in Miami for twenty years, and I stayed on Key
Biscayne whenever I went down there to visit. But
during that trip after the heart attack was the first time

 **I started to think that every
little twitch was another heart
attack. Any pain was a heart
attack. I was at the emergency
room three times—once in
March, once in April, once
in May.**

I found out where the Key Biscayne hospital was. First
thing I did when I got down there was to ask where the
hospital is in relation to the hotel. How could I get there
by myself if I had to? All kinds of paranoid thoughts
started cropping up while I was having this otherwise
good vacation. I was starting to feel a little spooked. You
know, everything is okay *now,* but something *could*
happen again at any time. I guess this was the flip side of
the years of denial.

When I got back to Washington the fear *really* hit.
Gut-wrenching fear. I was fearful that I'd go to sleep
and not wake up. So you do things like leave the TV on
deliberately. Leave the lights on deliberately. I was
afraid to be alone. Afraid I'd have another heart attack
and that would be *it.* I started to think that every little
twitch was another heart attack. Any pain was a heart
attack. I was at the emergency room three times—once
in March, once in April, once in May.

The first time it happened I was out at Capitol Center at a hockey game. I got a crick in my neck. It scared me so much that I left the game, got in the car, and drove straight to George Washington Hospital. Don't ask me why I did something as stupid as driving myself if I even *suspected* I was having a heart attack. Fear makes you

 I felt like a fool going to the emergency room for what turned out to be nothing. But they told me to never feel like that, always come in. *Never* deny your pain or ignore it 'cause you're afraid of feeling like a fool. That can kill you.

do some pretty stupid things. Anyway, I get to GW and they called Dr. Levy at home. He gets on the phone and says, "Larry, I really don't think you've got it. I'm gonna tell you, the odds are a hundred to one against your having a heart attack in the same place this quick. After an angioplasty, it doesn't make sense. You've got too much fluid flow. I'm not saying a year from now you won't get a buildup, but the odds are enormous, Larry. There is just no logic to it. But what does happen, since you've lost a lot of weight, your skin is closer to your bones and you're gonna get muscle pulls." And he said to take a nitroglycerin as a test, so I did. He says, "Obviously we hope this doesn't work, because if it works, it tells us it's the heart." It didn't work (thank God!) and they gave me muscle relaxants. Sent me home. I felt like a fool going to the emergency room for what turned out to be nothing. But they told me to never feel like that, always come in. *Never* deny your pain or ignore it 'cause you're afraid of feeling like a fool. That can kill you.

Warren Levy remembers that phone call he got when I had my first false alarm: "They called me at home and said, 'Larry King's in here again. He had some left-arm discomfort. We got an electrocardiogram, everything is normal, and you know, we think it's okay, but we want to admit him to be safe.' I went over the history and everything with the emergency room doctor and it just didn't sound like this was any great concern. But to make a long story short, the bottom line for them was saying, 'Hey, look, I don't want to be the person to send Larry King home from the emergency room and have him drop dead.' So I left home and went to the hospital." There's no question that sometimes it pays to be well known!

Levy recalls that he went in "because when you know a patient, and you've examined a patient, and you know his symptoms, it's just much easier to make any sort of decision than it is for someone who is seeing a patient for the first time. It's a very difficult position to be in in the emergency room. You see everyone for the first time at one point in time. It's not an enviable position. So I guess I came in about three o'clock in the morning and by then Larry was feeling fine, maybe with his tail between his legs a little bit, saying, 'Oh, gee whiz, you came all the way in here?' So we talked and I again tried to reassure him that I didn't think this symp-

'Hey, look, I don't want to be the person to send Larry King home from the emergency room and have him drop dead.'

tom he had had anything to do with his heart, but it was right for him to be aware of symptoms and not ignore them. On the one hand, you want patients not to be scared to death of everything they're feeling—on the other hand, you don't want patients to ignore real symptoms. You don't want them to start becoming deniers. And there was no better denier in the world than Larry King until the time he had his heart attack, and if his heart attack did anything, it turned him from a denier into a realist. Of course it should have been no surprise to Larry, because he knew he had cardiac disease. He knew he had cholesterol through the roof and he knew he wasn't doing a darned thing about it. As a matter of fact, one doctor who had treated Larry, when he was sure the heart attack was a mild one, told me, 'I think this is the best thing that could have happened to Larry. He's finally going to get his act together.' And he was absolutely right. It probably was the best thing that ever happened to Larry. In fact, he asked me that on the air when he had Dick Katz—my senior colleague from GW—and me on his show. He said, 'Well, here I am, I'm lucky, I had a small heart attack, I lived, things have gone well for me. Well, was this a good thing to happen to me? Am I fortunate that I had a heart attack?' I just turned around and asked him a question. I

said, 'Look, ever since we got here tonight you're telling us you've never felt better, you've lost weight,
you've stopped smoking, you're eating well, you feel
great, you feel like a new man, you feel thirty years
younger—so you tell me?'"

That's easy enough for the doctors to say. *They* don't
have to face that fear when the lights go off at night.
They don't have to lie there in the dark wondering if
their eyes will open in the morning. *They* don't have to
worry, "If I walk too fast, will I die? If I have sex, will I
die? If I carry my bags, will the pain come back?" Oh,
they tell you you're okay. They say you can do all these
things, but the fear is still there: "What if I wake up with
that pain again?" And I was always aware of where I
was in proximity to medical help. I would go on speaking engagements around the country and people would
drive me from the airport and I'd always notice the exit
that said "Hospital." I'd ask, in casual conversation,
"Where's the nearest hospital? How good is the ambu-
lance service here, do you know? How speedy is it?"
Because when you do speeches, you're in motels alone a
lot. And I always remember Levy telling me how lucky
I was to be having my heart attack in the hospital. A lot
of people live or die depending on where they have
their attack. I know it sounds crazy. But I went to three
or four group therapy sessions for heart attack patients
at GW and every one of the people there expressed the
same fears. So it may be crazy, but it's common crazy!

As the weeks go by, physically I'm feeling super. But
I'm having these fears. Fears and black depression. I
don't know what is causing it, other than fear of pain
and fear of dying.

Dr. Richard Katz on Fear and Depression

Most heart attack patients go through fears of one sort or another. In part it depends on what you're told when you leave the hospital. And what kind of person you are to begin with. Part of it's depression, and part's anxiety. Part of it's the issue of mortality, part of the issue is the great uncertainty of whether you can do what you used to do that made you happy. There's something depressing about that: Can you live freely without this cloud hanging over you? Then you start to analyze the "Why me? Did I do this to myself? Have I been hurting myself all this time? Am I to blame? Has my life-style been to blame? Has my fast-paced running around, not getting enough sleep, my high-stress life-style caused this?" And then you start blaming yourself for it and you know, most important of all was the smoking and the eating. There are many factors that are interacting in the development of heart disease, but you now recognize that you had some part in it. It wasn't just fate or genes. These are common questions, fears, and issues.

After a heart attack a lot of people retire who need not retire, but if that makes them happier, maybe that's a reflection of how they felt about the way their lives were, what their activities

> were. But sometimes they make a radical
> choice because they're misinformed.
> They're given the impression that they
> can't go back to work for six months, or
> that their jobs must be limited so that
> they can't continue to do them, and then
> they get depressed about that. How well
> they do afterward is extremely variable,
> and my sense has been that most active
> people do best by being directed back
> into that active life.

Well, I was definitely getting back into my active life. I never gave a second's thought to slowing down or retiring. I just started with the radio show and then a week later went back on television. Of course I cut the radio show back by an hour, going from 11 P.M. to 3 A.M. instead of 11 to 4. I went to group therapy sessions for heart patients for about a month. I found I really didn't like the concept, but I was there long enough to discover that there was *nothing* unique about what I was experiencing. And I also discovered that time and reality were the only effective antidotes to the fear. The longer I survived without experiencing the pain, the less I feared it, and death. So bit by bit the fears subsided. First I was able to turn the TV off—sleep without that reassuring noise. Then came the lights. I guess the trick was realizing two things: I really did seem to be better, and sleeping with the lights and TV on wasn't ultimately going to make a bit of difference except to the electric company. I realize now that this initial adjustment was particularly difficult for me because I was

I also discovered that time and reality were the only effective antidotes to the fear. The longer I survived without experiencing the pain, the less I feared it, and death.

alone. I had my daughter, Chaia, but I certainly didn't want to burden her with all my fears—although I'm sure I did. But it was basically just me and the fears. The doctors tell me that it all might have been a good deal easier if I'd had someone to share my anxiety with. But of course that person—spouse, lover, whatever—has to be aware of what's happening so that they're not overwhelmed by it all. I suppose that I should have made greater use of the counseling available to me. And many cities have post-heart attack programs available for spouses—and what they're now calling "significant others"—and based on my experience, I think these programs could provide a couple with a great deal of help in the initial period of adjustment.

4

Back to Work

I THINK THE FIRST TWO QUESTIONS ANY HEART AT-
tack patient asks—after "Am I gonna live?"—are "How
soon can I go back to work?" and "What about sex?" At
my age the sex question was certainly important, but
the work question came first. As I was leaving the hospital they said I could go back to work in three weeks, but
I decided on four. The doctors at GW told me pretty
much what I've heard from every doctor now: "Your
work is sedentary. You know, you're not chopping wood
for a living." So since my job isn't physically demand-
ing, the only other question was the level of stress involved.

It's sure no secret that I'm a classic "Type A": hard-
driving, constantly on the go, extremely time-con-
scious, uptight when my environment gets out of my
control—you know the symptoms. But the interesting
thing is that I'm very relaxed about my work. In fact, I
wouldn't be exaggerating to say that while I take my
work very seriously, it's my relaxation. It doesn't make
me uptight at all. I know some people find it hard to
believe that I could be in front of a live mike, or camera,

with literally millions of people watching or listening, and not be nervous. But what is there to be nervous about? A guest doesn't show up? I take phone calls. A guest freezes on me or just doesn't come across well? I go to the phones. I like working the phones. I do it well. It's fun. So my work is strain-free. In fact, Richard Katz commented on that fact after he and Dr. Levy were on my show after the heart attack.

"Larry knows how to ask questions and he's very curious without having any insecurity about not being knowledgeable in an area where he's talking to a so-called expert," says Katz. "When we went on his radio show he was obviously very relaxed and ran through the hours very smoothly. I was impressed by that and it confirmed the sense that I got about him that this was a relaxing form of activity for him. You know, you hear the stories about what happens when people are forced to retire—how they just vegetate and they die. And then there is the variation on that theme that you cut back someone's work, if that work provides the enjoyment in their life, if it's their avocation as well as their vocation, and you're doing them a disservice. The old person says, 'Better I should die.'

"I tried, unsuccessfully, to get Larry into a cardiac rehabilitation program. Because in a program you get more time with health professionals and patients who've been through this, and you see these old guys doing all this stuff you're afraid you can't do. And there's time for questions to be answered by my nurses who are in the rehab program. I felt sorry that Larry couldn't have the advantage of that, because I can spend only so much time with patients."

When I talked to David Blumenthal, my cardiologist

in New York, he made many of the same comments. He
also stressed the fact that "if you take the honest-to-God
Type A and try to turn him into anything else, you'll
have a very unhappy person. And I don't even try. I
would try with people who are extreme, who do lunatic
kinds of things. But for someone like Larry, who basically says, 'I'm very good at what I do. I work hard at
what I do. I'm very successful at what I do,' I say, fine,
okay. Even his weird hours are okay. As long as his
hormones are shifted a little bit. They catch up for him.
If he worked the schedule every other day, so his body
couldn't adjust, that would be a problem. I would consider that unacceptable. I'm much more unhappy with
the policeman who works day shifts, night shifts, medium shifts every three weeks than I am with Larry. Or
I'm more unhappy with the guy who travels all over the
place back and forth, changing time zones all the time,
than I am with someone like Larry, who says, 'Okay,
this is what my schedule is. It's stable, it's just that it's
shifted eight hours from everybody else's.' "

All the doctors had told me that, basically, I could go
back to work as soon as I felt up to it. So I picked a date.
I wanted to go back to television sooner, but radio in-
sisted that I come back to them. And since they were
paying me more then, they wanted me back the same
night or earlier.

Well, anyway, it was great. My special friend Angie
Dickinson flew in to be there the first night I was back.
Ironically, the show was March 24—one month from
the day of the heart attack. And even more ironic was
the fact that my first guest was Dr. Frank Young, the
commissioner of the Food and Drug Administration.
He'd been my guest on television the last show before

the heart attack. Anyway, we talked about AIDS and we discussed AIDS and AZT. Young asked me about tPA because he knew I had taken it in the hospital. He told me he was sure they were going to approve that fairly shortly, which actually took them some time. First guest back on the radio was some rock star who Angie knew. Angie introduced me back on the radio show and she said, "Now, ladies and gentlemen, here's Larry." It was all very nice.

 Heart attack or not, I don't think most people could fathom Larry King not smoking.

I don't think anyone was particularly nervous about me or my health when I went back to work. At least they didn't show it if they were. Everyone was extremely nice. There were flowers and "Welcome Home's" and open arms . . . they were wonderful. I think that if anything about me seemed odd or different to people, it was the fact that I wasn't smoking. People kept saying to me they couldn't believe that I wasn't smoking. I mean, here I am, a guy who'd never even tried to quit. I leave work one night a cigarette hanging out of my mouth, have a heart attack, and return a month later not smoking. Heart attack or not, I don't think most people could fathom Larry King not smoking. But when I came back I just sensed a warmth, a good feeling, and a sense of "This guy ain't smoking!"

Of course the other thing that might have struck people as odd was that I looked very good—much better than I had before I'd left. I mean, I might have had a heart attack, but I'd been in Florida, gotten tan, lost weight, stopped smoking. Everyone said I looked fantastic.

5
Sex and the Psyche

AS I'VE ALREADY MENTIONED, YOU SURVIVE A HEART attack, one of the first things you want to know is, "What about sex? Can I have it? Will it hurt? Is it safe? Do I need to do anything special, positions?" Whatever. You're scared: scared that you won't be able to resume whatever level of sexual activity you enjoyed before the heart attack; scared that if you do resume it, you'll experience that pain again. You have to remember, for me and many heart patients one of the first ways you know you're in trouble is you start having pain during sex. You start slowly, everything's fine. Things start to get going, your heart calls for more oxygen, and—wham! It hurts. So you can get to the point where you associate sex and angina. Then after you've had your heart attack, it's almost impossible not to wonder if you're going to end up associating sex and death. I mean, sex is great. I've always thought of myself as a very sexual person. Even with my schedule and being single, at age fifty-four I figure I was having sex about two, three times a week. Loved it. It had always been important to me. But I certainly wasn't prepared to die for it.

When I left the hospital I asked, "When can I have sex?"

The last thing they do for you when you leave the

 I'm thinking, "Can I perform? Will I perform? Will I be in pain? Will I have sex? What will it be like?"

hospital after a heart attack is give you all your prescriptions and make an appointment for you for a checkup. Then they say, "Good-bye, see you in three months." And they ask if you have any questions. I said, "Well, the usual. Sex. When can I have it?" And Katz said, "What we tell you is, treat sex like a flight of stairs. For the first week at home you try not to go up the stairs at all. The second week you go up the stairs gingerly. The third week you just go up the stairs." So with sex I translated that to mean the first week it's nothing. The second week I regarded "gingerly" as meaning masturbation. And the third week out of the hospital was for climbing the "stairs" normally.

But even after talking to the doctors, I'm thinking, "Can I perform? Will I perform? Will I be in pain? Will I have sex? What will it be like?" I never considered that I might have a life without sex. Although, I'll tell you, at that time I was still so scared of possibly having to have bypass surgery at some point that if they had given me a choice—"Give up all sex for the rest of your life and you'll live perfectly comfortably and won't need surgery" or "Have surgery and live comfortably and have sex"—I'd have given it up in a minute. But I never thought I'd have to live a celibate life. So my worry wasn't that I wouldn't have sex—the worry was whether it was going to hurt when I did have sex.

What's interesting is that for all the heart patient's fear of sex, the act itself really puts very little stress on the heart. I was talking to Dr. Edward Brown, a research cardiologist at the State University of New York at Stony Brook, and he told me that there have been studies done that show that, in terms of the heart, sex doesn't involve much work. Believe it or not, the blood pressure goes up a bit, the pulse rises a little, and the oxygen consumption of the heart goes up some, but the amount of increase is comparatively slight. Certainly not enough to put anything that could be called strain on a relatively healthy heart. Now if you're already having angina, those small increases may be enough to cause pain. But at the time you go home from the hospital, and usually you've had some form of major treatment to control the angina, sex doesn't really affect things much. As long as the partner's your wife or an old partner! No kidding. They've also found that sex with a new partner, or sex with a partner other than your spouse—if you're married—definitely affects the heart more than sex with a regular partner.

But I didn't know any of that at the time I left the hospital. I was even afraid of masturbating, even though they'd told me to start back to sex with that, and even though you use masturbation as a very convenient way to give you some indication of what having intercourse is gonna be like. But it's not the same as intercourse because you're controlling it more. There's no

Your mind ain't on the thing at hand. Your mind is on "Am I gonna live?"

emotional high with masturbation; it's never the same. But it is something. So for two weeks after leaving the hospital I didn't do anything. And then one night I masturbated. I knew that the first time I did it the trick was to do it very slowly. They had told me that this was the intelligent way to go about it. And that went fine.

A week later I had intercourse for the first time since the heart attack. And that first time I had sex I was *so* afraid. Afraid that the pain would come again. But it didn't. And finally . . . you know, it just wasn't exciting because it was always on my mind: you know, how badly it might damage my muscle, and whether my artery could do this. That's what I kept thinking about. It was just plain scary. I kept thinking, "Is this gonna hurt? Is that gonna hurt?" You need a woman who is gonna be very much the aggressor, because keeping it up is not gonna be easy because your mind is elsewhere. Your mind ain't on the thing at hand. Your mind is on "Am I gonna live?" But once I past the first time, I never thought about it again. I found out in the couple of times that I went to group therapy that these are very common fears and worries. *Everyone* in the group had 'em. But once I got past that first time, I was home free. I think that, in part, that had to do with the fact that I was walking every day. I say that for two reasons: The first is that the doctors tell me that the better your physical condition, the easier—and more enjoyable—

sex will be. I was walking a lot—built up to a few miles a day—so I probably figured that if I could walk a couple of miles and not only survive but feel good, then I could probably do fine in bed. And, second, I figured that if I could take those walks without pain, I could have sex without pain.

Another thing I realized is that it helps to have a partner who's a friend as well as a lover. The first time I had sex after the heart attack it was with this woman in Miami who's a close friend. Friend, lover, confidante. We could talk about it. She'd say, you know, "What do you want me to do? What can I do to help? If you have any pain, let's talk about it." That kind of thing. I wasn't romancing her and trying to impress her. That was wonderful. It was relaxed. Of course you can have that with a spouse too. But the doctors tell me that sometimes the wife is more scared of post-heart attack sex than her husband is—and *he* had the heart attack. There's this fear on the part of the woman that she'll cause pain. Hell, she may be afraid she'll kill her husband. So that's something that the couple absolutely has to talk about. Otherwise, the doctors say, the husband and wife may end up not having any sex and each will blame it on the other. And as a veteran of two marriages, I can tell you that that kind of thing doesn't help the heart at all!

You know, it's funny, but after I didn't have pain the first couple of times I had sex, the fear disappeared completely. Didn't think about it at all. But then, late summer, early fall, the angina started back, and one of the first times it showed up was during sex. I started getting bad angina. Same as running through an airport. Right in the middle of sex. I'd have to stop. Take a

As I began to experience pain during sex I found I was less likely to have it. That's when I knew I was getting into trouble again.

pill. The woman I was dating at the time got scared. This was around Labor Day. We were staying in a hotel at the beach. She said something like, "Oh no, you're not gonna have a heart attack here at the beach." But I finished, went back and finished. I talked to my doctors about it and they told me to take a Nitrostat *before* sex, as a prophylactic for my heart. But even so, as I began to experience pain during sex I found I was less likely to have it. That's when I *knew* I was getting into trouble again.

6

Smoking, Diet, and Exercise

IF THERE WAS ONE THING THAT THE HEART ATTACK made clear to me, it was that I had to make some changes in the way I was living. Had to. No question. The only question was exactly what changes to make and how to make them. Of course, to be realistic about it, there was also the unspoken question of whether I could make the changes. But at the time I think I simply thought I *would* do it. I mean, my life-style was not exactly a model for anyone—at least not for anyone who wanted to live to his allotted three score and ten.

To start with, there was the matter of cigarettes. A cigarette was as much a part of me as anything. Started smoking when I was seventeen. Thirty-six years, two, three packs a day. Call it two and a half packs a day and it works out to 638,750 cigarettes. Smoking was as much a part of my life as eating, sleeping, or sex. I smoked through every facet of life. Through showers. Through sex. When you really smoke a lot, you learn how to smoke in every situation. Edward R. Murrow told me he lit one cigarette a day, the first one, and every old one lit a new one. And Edward R. Murrow couldn't stop—until lung cancer finally got him. I always knew it wasn't good for me. Just couldn't stop. The rewards were too great. It just felt good to smoke. And I could smoke anytime, anywhere. I knew ways to keep it in a soap dish. So you take it into the shower. God, how many times I had four going at once. You know, answer the phone, put it down over there. And then go into another room, light up another one in there. I used to think, "How could you talk on the phone and not smoke? How could you write and not smoke? How could you broadcast and not smoke? How could you fly in an airplane and not smoke? How could you have a meal and not smoke? How could you make love and not smoke?" I just couldn't understand it. Just the way people can't understand how I quit.

You know, if I hadn't had the heart attack, I never would have quit. I had no desire to live without smoking. Hell, I'd known for seven years that I had heart disease. I'd known that was what killed my father. But somehow none of that had any real effect on me. My doctors had been telling me to quit. My daughter, Chaia, had been telling me to quit—in fact, she had started smoking, and I *know* that was because of me. And I had certainly read enough to know that smoking is a major contributing factor to coronary artery disease. But still I couldn't even think about quitting. *Wouldn't* think about it.

So now everybody asks me, "Larry, what's your secret? How did you do it? How'd you quit at all, let alone cold turkey?" You know what? It's no secret and it was no big deal: I was scared to death. I fit that term: scared to death. You lie there on that hospital gurney, everybody rushing around you in the emergency room, and

You lie there on that hospital gurney, everybody rushing around you in the emergency room, and you hear the doctor say, "Mr. King, you are having a heart attack." Hell, you got half a brain in your head, that's the instant you quit. You say, "I ain't goin' through *this* again! Not for some damn cigarettes."

you hear the doctor say, "Mr. King, you are having a heart attack." Hell, you got half a brain in your head, that's the instant you quit. You say, "I ain't goin' through *this* again! Not for some damn cigarettes." And that's that. I haven't even thought about having one since. I don't mind if people around me smoke. You know, I don't dwell on it because I understand it. I'm not angry at the smoker. Don't look down at the smoker. If it was healthy, I'd be first on line. It's a wonderful thing to do with your hands. It feels good. If the tobacco tastes good, it's marvelous. I can even understand a guy like Martin Sheen, who had a far worse heart attack than mine—they didn't give him any chance. But he still smokes. Bob Fosse? Smoked five packs of Camels a day. And that's where I thought I'd be, always a smoker. But the time came, and that was that. I'm not a smoker. Period.

Started smoking when I was seventeen. Thirty-six years, two, three packs a day. Call it two and a half packs a day and it works out to 638,750 cigarettes.

Now, trying to change my diet? That was another matter. You may not believe this, but it was much harder than giving up smoking. Oh, I did it. Made a radical change. It was harder than cigarettes, but it wasn't impossible because I was so scared. See, I used that period of fear to do everything. Lost weight, stopped smoking, changed my diet. But that was the time I was leaving the television and lights on when I slept. And the man who does *that* is not going to light up a cigarette or eat a piece of bacon. He's too scared.

I used to eat a pretty awful diet, and eat in pretty weird ways. I'd get up around 9:30 A.M. and have a bagel, cream cheese, coffee, cream and sugar, read the paper. Two cigarettes before any of this. Cigarettes in the bathroom. Cigarette dangling out of my mouth as I pick up the *Washington Post.* Hang around, drive into the city, lunch. Lunch would be steak, some home fries. Can't have a steak without the home fries. No walking. Get into the car, drive back home, do a column, read a book, relax, eat early. If I didn't eat early, I'd go to the radio network, order some pizza. In 1985, when I started to do the TV show, I started to change my eating habits a bit. I started eating fried rice, Chinese food. I like Chinese food. In short, my diet was pretty appall-

You give up smoking, you give up one pleasure, one habit. You radically alter your diet and you give up literally dozens of pleasures and habits. But you want to live badly enough, you simply do what you've got to do.

ing. I ate what I felt like, when I felt like it. It was about as balanced as a seesaw with a fat man on one end. It included few if any vegetables, little in the way of fiber, and it was heavy with red meat, saturated fats of all kinds. I had a diet that would drive a dietitian to smoke.

I know that many people will find it hard to believe that I found it easier to give up smoking than to change my diet. But think about it: Not only is eating as enjoyable as smoking, it has few, if any, of the more obvious drawbacks of smoking. You can eat all the awful things you like and not gain weight—as long as you don't overdo it. You're encouraged, rather than discouraged, to eat at virtually every kind of social function. And we all associate certain foods with pleasurable times and events in our lives: What is an ice-cream sundae but a time machine back to a warm summer day when you were a kid? What is a stack of pancakes swimming in butter and syrup but a winter Sunday morning in your mother's kitchen? And, even more obvious, you give up smoking, you give up one pleasure, one habit. You radically alter your diet and you give up literally dozens of pleasures and habits. But you want to live badly enough, you simply do what you've got to do.

Still, I know there were some changes I made in my life that really surprised the doctors: like the way I gave up smoking. Katz says he was particularly surprised about that because it's very difficult for a lot of chain-smokers, heavy smokers, to give it up. We're really psychologically—and physically—addicted to smoking. And I just kicked it. Even more remarkable, said Katz, is that a lot of smokers who quit substitute eating for something to have in their mouths. I not only kicked the oral habit of smoking, but I lost weight—went on a terrific diet and lost weight and became a real convert. I mean, before the heart attack I was at least fifteen pounds overweight. But afterwards I lost between fifteen and twenty pounds—got down to my recommended weight. And you want to know my secret? The Larry King Matzoh Diet. That's right. Matzoh. Unleavened bread. Jewish saltless saltines. I'd keep a box in the apartment. At work. Want to eat something, I'd just eat some matzoh. They're low in calories. Low in sodium. Fill the mouth and kill the hunger. Try it. You're in a restaurant, try asking for matzoh or saltless crackers. You can't get that, eat some of the bread or rolls, but *not* the butter. You want to use carrot or celery sticks instead, I can't stop you. But if you want to really succeed at changing your eating, remember, it's The Larry King Matzoh Diet.

Of course, Katz points out that as well as I did in giving up smoking and improving my diet—I haven't had red meat since the heart attack—I didn't take his advice about joining a cardiac rehabilitation program at GW. Somehow I just never found the time to do it.

Guess I didn't want to. Don't know why. Some people have suggested that I avoided it because I didn't want to think of myself as an "invalid," a "cardiac cripple." But I don't think that was it 'cause I think of myself as a heart patient just as much as I think of myself as an ex-smoker. Am now and always will be.

But, as Katz says, "About six to eight weeks after a heart attack, I often recommend a cardiac rehabilitation program for a patient like Larry, one of a variety of types, and that takes a certain amount of time and scheduling and discipline in a different way for individuals. We talked about it off and on and I sensed a reluctance on his part. He immediately began to follow instructions on my part regarding exercise, and went out and took walks and felt quite good with that and was making a point of going out and doing that. But for whatever reasons, he was reluctant to participate in a cardiac rehabilitation program at GW. I even suggested that he just do it for a month in a supervised session and then he could continue on his own, which I do with many patients because of scheduling issues. We set that up, but he backed out of that, pulled out indefinitely.

"I don't know why Larry backed out," Katz says, "whether he had scheduling problems or he just didn't want to be with a group of people who also were 'sick' and had heart disease. He also told me that he was depressed at that point, he felt lonely to some degree, and I think he was close to being scared. It may be that at that point he was, for the first time, more realistically facing the fact that he really had serious heart disease. He had certainly been told before that he had coronary artery disease, but he had never had a heart attack before. And there's something about those words that had a great meaning: For the first time he was really facing his own mortality. I think that paralyzed him in a sense. Yet on the other hand, he was able to do all the other things."

Warren Levy, the cardiologist who took care of me the morning of the heart attack, notes that most people don't make the kind of "radical" changes that I made. "I am usually happy if I can get someone to stop smoking," says Levy. "To me that is a victory, because I personally feel that it is the single best thing anyone can do following a heart attack to reduce their risk of a recurring event, or at least to extend their life expectancy. With patients like Larry, who do have high cholesterols, you need to work with them much harder to get their cholesterols down, to change their eating habits, and that's usually a very difficult thing to change. I guess folks fall into two schools: There's the sort of denier school, the group that says, 'Okay, it happened, but now I'm okay. I'm going back to work, everything is going to be fine.' And then there's the realist school, the group that says, 'I'm just lucky to have survived this. If I want to take advantage of it, I'm going to have to do some serious work now.' The odd thing is that, from what I've been able to determine, prior to the heart attack, Larry was the headmaster of the denier school. But that heart attack really turned him around."

Then there's Chaia. She used to smoke—I'm sure because I did. Now she doesn't. She watches her diet. Maybe it's not perfect, but it's better than it was. I didn't realize it at the time, but I think she had a lot of anger over the fact that I wasn't taking care of myself before the heart attack. In talks we've had since, she's told me that every time she'd go to see Gabe Merkin—

we both used the same internist—he'd be on her about how she had to get me to quit smoking and clean up my act. And that must have been hard on her.

Chaia was worried because my behavior was reckless. She saw it as reckless and immature. Everybody is reckless to a certain point. She thought I was reckless throughout my life until I couldn't be anymore. Now I had to face the music.

Just as it amazes people that I made it to fifty-four, I find it amazing that Herbie Cohen made it that far. Not only were our hereditary risk factors similar, our horrendous life-styles were almost identical. It's wonderful what my heart attack did for Herbie.

"When I saw Larry in the hospital, having known Larry for so many years, and . . . I mean, I have a very close relationship with Larry, and when you see someone in a situation like that, I think it has a big impact on you. After his heart attack, he's changing his life-style—he's not smoking anymore—and I'm still smoking ten, fifteen cigars a day. I was addicted. Badly. I'm not exercising either. I remember going for my physical and they tell me, 'You have to exercise, you have to walk.' In fact, 'the highlight of your day,' the doctor said to me, 'should be walking. You should look forward to your walk.' So I come home and tell my wife, 'From now on, the highlight of my day is going to be walking. I'm going to get up in the morning and I'm going to say, "Oh boy, I can hardly wait to walk. Can hardly wait to get out there in the wind chill factor of forty below zero in Chicago. Get out there and walk, highlight of my day." ' So, you know, the doctor would tell me that, but I didn't do it. Now, after Larry's heart attack, I said, 'All

right, I'm going to have to change *my* life.' Larry's
heart attack gave me some impetus to change. I said,
'First thing I'm going to do is I'm going to stop smoking,
because I can't go on like this.' And I stopped smoking.

"It wasn't just the cigars I gave up. I mean something
really happened to me when I saw Larry lying there. I
knew that five years ago my triglycerides were very
high, my cholesterol was very high. I didn't do anything
about it. One thing was that I didn't have any symptoms
at all of heart disease: No pain. No angina. EKG was
normal. So I began to realize when I saw Larry's situation, and the fact that my father was fifty when he had
his first heart attack—lived to eighty-three, though!—
that it wasn't really fair to those I love for me to have
that kind of attitude about living and my health when I
have responsibilities. You know, people rely on you and
I began to realize I had an obligation to myself and
others to take care of myself. So starting in July, five
months after Larry's heart attack, I said, 'Hey, now that
I've got the smoking out of the way, I don't do that
anymore, I'm going to exercise and do this walking and
lose weight.' I was able to lose weight and walk and I
was doing great until the winter came in Chicago.
There was no way I was gonna keep going out in that
ungodly weather, so I had to get a treadmill. But using
that is really hard—it's such a bore—so the biggest
problem was continuing to exercise regularly, but I did
it.

"My stress-test report was really good. Now I can jog
ninety minutes! I became crazy for a while. As my wife
says about me, what makes me successful in work is that
I'm single-minded and tenacious and persistent, and
that carries over in personality—I'm a compulsive,

crazy person. And when I smoked cigars, I chain-smoked cigars. When I ate, I ate. And then when I decided I was going to be healthy, I got healthy. I mean, my resting pulse is about fifty-four, fifty-seven now, which is pretty incredible for a fifty-four-year-old guy."

What I found particularly interesting, in talking to David Blumenthal later, is that he said that "it's not as uncommon as you would think for people to make the kind of radical life-style changes that both you and Herbie made. Even giving up smoking the way you did isn't that unusual. Part of it is, of course, the fact that you're hospitalized. You don't have the opportunity to smoke, so already you've got a leg up on kicking the habit. You get through those first eight or ten days, which are among the hardest, and you haven't got any choice. And, as you noted, you're scared stiff: If you're appropriately scared stiff, you tend not to want to smoke. One of the dilemmas though—and luckily you don't have this problem—is when you have a spouse who smokes. That, to me, is the hardest. And I am usually furious with the spouse when they won't stop smoking. You know, here they are, here's their loved one, they're all so concerned and saying 'What can I do?' and this and that, and then you say, 'He stopped smoking, it'll be a lot easier at home if you don't smoke.' And then the spouse can't stop or won't stop. That I find, of all things, the most incredible.

"But you'd be surprised how many heart attack victims will initially stop," David tells me. "The dilemma is more that they'll stray later, rather than get the quick, permanent stop. It's not as hard in the hospital, we'll sedate you—there are people coming in and they're anxious, they get some Valium, they don't have the opportunity to smoke. It's a function of willpower—some have it, some don't. I'm sure when you ask them, 'Do you ever feel like smoking?' they answer, 'All the time, every minute.' Which I basically can't relate to as a nonsmoker.

"You know, I watch these people running around . . . most of those people will change their life-style in the sense that they'll do things right—maybe they'll exercise more, maybe not. But most end up working the way they did before. I'm not so sure that's necessarily terrible if the work is truly important to them. Sometimes cutting back can be more stressful. I don't think it's necessarily bad for people to make phone calls related to business while they're in the hospital, or even to conduct occasional meetings. The stress of thinking your business is going down the drain, the stress generated by thinking you're losing some account can be a lot worse than the strain of working. I certainly put a lot of limits on patients, particularly in the beginning. I'll say, 'You may only go in to work from ten to eleven. At eleven I'm going to make your wife come and get you. You can't be there in an open-ended fashion.' For these guys, to go in, answer four phone calls, open the mail, and things like that frequently is happier and better for them. I had one guy who basically was going nuts at home and was really having a lot of problems. Finally I said, 'Go to work for a few hours,' and he was great—all of the craziness melted away, all the fears he had of separation and stuff like that—he got back into his usual environment, loved what he did, and he felt a lot better. I'm not so big on making people change unless what they're doing is self-destructive. I don't mind people working hard, as long as it's not at the expense of everything else. There's a great deal about this Type A/Type B stuff we just don't understand. But the temptation when someone goes back to working from 7 A.M. to 7 P.M. is to send out for lunch, send out for dinner. You send out—what are you gonna get? Corned beef? What do you get in for dinner? Pizza? And everybody's smoking cigarettes and drinking a lot of coffee. That's where the bind is. But if an individual has the self-discipline to say, 'Wait, we're sending out for the deli, I'll either have a can of tuna or I'll have a turkey sandwich,' that's not such a big deal for me. So what? So you work hard."

David and practically every other doctor I've talked to about this pointed out that we—and that *we* often includes doctors—seem to forget that medicine is still an art. Doctors know a lot, but there's a lot more they don't know. We go to the doctor and say, "Come on, Doc, give it to me straight. . . ." Problem is, there may not be a "straight." So then you get all kinds of "we think's," and "we believe's," and "but there's always the chances." You know, if you're going to a good doctor, he's going to remember enough of his scientific training to remember that there are no absolutes. For instance, if you asked an engineer if it was absolutely safe for you to cross the George Washington Bridge from New York to New Jersey, he'd tell you, "Of course it's safe, but there is always a statistically significant chance that the bridge will collapse while you're on it. It's possible, but *extremely* unlikely." He can't give you an *absolute* guarantee. So is that gonna keep you from going to Jersey to visit your sister? No way. Well, medicine's like that. They just can't guarantee that this treatment or that will work, or how much of a good thing's bad for you, or how much of a bad thing's good. Take coffee, for example. One day you hear it causes cancer. Then they say it doesn't. One day it's bad for heart patients. The next day it's okay. Now, David tells me, most researchers and cardiologists think it might be okay to have up to two cups a day. They don't really know what happens after that. Might be okay, might not. They think that coffee *probably* raises cholesterol a little bit, and it certainly raises the pulse rate, so why take a chance? Stick to the two-cup limit, says David.

 You know the seat-belt commercial where the cop says, "I've never unbuckled a dead person"? Well, David says, "Every time I've seen a young man with a heart attack—he's always been a smoker." Without exception.

Problem is, even if your life's at stake, there's just so much change you can make—just so much each person's capable of. It varies, of course. I was able to make really major changes in the areas of smoking, diet, and exercise. But I can't really modify my stressful behavior. In fact, I was probably able to make the changes I did make *because* I'm such a Type A. It's like Herbie says: We're both so intense about whatever we do that if what we're doing is "modifying" some behavior, boy! We modify it to a fare-thee-well.

But David says that a good doctor has to realize that, for most people, there are limits as to how much you can get them to change. He says the doctor has to sort of pick and choose—figure out what the fights are going to be. His biggest fight is always cigarettes. Says that's the number-one thing that *must* be eliminated. Above bad foods. You know the seat-belt commercial where the cop says, "I've never unbuckled a dead person"? Well, David says, "Every time I've seen a young man with a heart attack—he's always been a smoker." Without exception. Young meaning under forty. A lot of it will be in the forties—always smokers—so that's always battle number one, without question. He says battle number two is diet, getting that cholesterol down, no question. Exercise comes after that because there's less scientific evidence to show exactly what the benefit is. No question that exercise makes you feel better, able to do more, able to feel better about yourself because you're contributing to your health, but they don't know if it's going to make a major impact on your life, the way not smoking or changing your diet is.

So what they *really* want you to do is have this three-point program: You stop smoking; you eat right; you go out and exercise—you're taking a major role in your health. That's good, it makes you feel more in control of your life, makes it easier to withstand the temptation of bad things. You *know* you're making a major difference in your own health.

7
Taking Stock

YOU HAVE A HEART ATTACK, FIRST THING YOU THINK is, "I gotta change my life." You know that saying "Today is the first day of the rest of your life?" Well, you survive a heart attack and that's it: The day after really *is* the first day of the rest of your life. What you don't know is how long that life's gonna be. All of a sudden you gotta deal with the fact that you *are* gonna die one of these days. Death becomes real. And if death is real, then you absolutely have to make the most of what time you've got.

First thing you do, if you smoke, you give up smoking. You're a couch potato, you start exercising. You live on steak, you switch to fish and broiled chicken without the skin. You do all the obvious stuff. Do what the doctor tells you to do. But it goes much deeper than that. You teeter on the edge of the abyss and you don't fall in, you're gonna think long and hard about what life means to you, what the people in your life mean, and what you're gonna do about that. Problem is, you're reassessing things when you're scared to death, so the conclusions you come to aren't necessarily the world's best.

You're likely to think that whatever your life wasn't it ought to be. And whatever it was is what caused your heart attack. If you're a hardworking family man with a wife, three kids, dog, cat, crabgrass, and a station wagon, you think maybe you should trade it all in for a blonde, a Corvette, and some gold chains. On the other hand, you're a guy like me—traveling all the time, working weird hours, in the spotlight—you think maybe what you need is to settle down, find Miss Right, and slow down. Do the pipe-and-slippers bit. So that's what I set out to do.

Soon after the heart attack I began a serious pursuit of my second ex-wife, Sharon King. This began during the period when I was sleeping with the lights and the television on at night. I was afraid to be alone. I wanted someone beside me. I wanted someone I knew, was familiar with. I had a wide choice of new people. But I wanted somebody old, familiar. And Sharon fit the bill. Of course, in retrospect, I realize that the whole thing was crazy from the beginning. I mean, Sharon and I had been married for six years and divorced for five. We got divorced because we couldn't stay married. We had some wonderful times, but we just couldn't work things out. And there was really no reason to think that we could just because I'd had a heart attack. I also realize now that what really attracted me was the quest—the idea of winning her back. Once the quest was over, it was no longer interesting. But I see all this in retrospect. Didn't see it at the time.

Prior to the heart attack I was very happy living alone. I was totally my own master. I wanted to see someone, I'd see them. Didn't want to, I wouldn't. Want to go to a ball game? I'd go. No one to ask. No one to think about. But then when I had the heart attack, I began thinking about the fact that we all give up things for certain other things.

 Every person who's ever had a heart attack knows they're gonna die. But what you find out eventually is your values —who you are—really haven't changed, they've just been modified a bit.

I thought that what I wanted was the kind of relationship where I wake up in the morning with the same person every day. But I've found over the years that that hasn't worked for me. I think one of the reasons it doesn't work is that I don't give to it. And I think one of the reasons I don't give to it is that I'm very much a this-is-what-I-want-to-do person.

But I was really convinced in those first months that I wanted to be with someone. That I didn't want to be alone. That I wanted a life where there were things more important than work. I wanted someone to share things with. I didn't realize that not only was I probably choosing the wrong person but also affecting all those others in my life who cared about me. For instance, my daughter didn't like Sharon, so I had problems with my daughter. I didn't handle the whole thing very well with Chaia. I was honest, but I didn't handle it very well.

Still, I was somehow convinced that, because I'd had a heart attack, things would work out where they hadn't worked before. Why? Because my values were different—or so I thought. Nobody's ever completely the same after a heart attack. You can't be the same. You've had a traumatic experience and you can't deny it. Every person who's ever had a heart attack knows they're gonna die. But what you find out eventually is your values—who you are—really haven't changed, they've just been modified a bit.

Anyway, I convince myself that I need Sharon. And I set out to get her as only I can set out to get something. I'm sending flowers. Gifts. The whole bit. Sharon was very hesitant to respond to the chase, in part because we'd been through it before, because we had been seeing each other on and off over the years after we were divorced. Well, we'd break off, it never worked. Sometimes she chased me. Sometimes I chased her. I said the difference was that I was very honest, I had had a heart attack, and I figured things had changed. She was seeing a guy at the time. I don't know how much that motivated me. It sure played a part. The desire of success, a victory.

Of course, what I should have been thinking about was why we split up in the first place and whether or not anything would really be any different. Sharon and I are very different people: I'm very loose with a dollar; Sharon's very tight with a dollar. I'm very lenient with children; Sharon's very strict with children. I'm very risk-taking; Sharon is non-risk-taking. And we each admired those traits in each other—up to a point. We had a great physical attraction. A great physical relationship. She's outstandingly pretty. But we got on each

other's nerves. When we got mad, I mean, I hated her.
It wasn't just dislike, it was hate. And when we broke up
it was bitter. We both made a lot of mistakes. So this
time, in the chase, I was the chaser. And the chasee was
playing a tough game. The chasee dated me, but the
chasee was still seeing this other guy. The chasee was
playing it cool. Until one day the chaser stopped.

I was involved in this thing because I was envisioning
the world's perfect life; that Chaia would forgive all the
previous things that have happened; that I was step-
ping into making a lot of money. We would live in a
palace; a home in L.A. and a home in Washington. Jet-
travel and do wonderful things. But Sharon continued,
in my opinion, to still be herself and I continued to still
be me. Even though she cared, she still saw this other
guy, who she really liked, who was very nice to her
family. And one day he did her a favor and drove her
somewhere—after I thought they had stopped seeing
each other. And I passed them on the road. It wasn't
romantic. I don't believe it was romantic, but that
didn't matter. But what happened was a wonderful
thing. I was angry and started to get all those jealous
kinds of things. And suddenly, like the heavens opened
up, I stopped caring. I said, "I don't give a damn. I don't
care. I just don't care." And that, for me, was the end of
that. On with the next phase of my life—except for the
fact that it had taken six months for me to get to that
point, and, in the meantime, I had hurt Chaia, and my
friends were angry because they didn't like Sharon, and
I had driven a lot of other people in my life crazy.

Before the heart attack, and since, I'd been seeing
Angie Dickinson for quite some time, and there was
always the question of why I didn't pursue her after the

heart attack the way I did Sharon. I guess the answer to that is twofold: In the first place, Sharon represented something special to me—continuity, family, home and hearth. Shouldn't have, but she did. The other thing was that Angie and I didn't live in the same city—or even on the same coast. See, if Angie had lived in the same city, and we had been together after the heart attack, and let that grow, we could have had a very nice marriage. I'm not saying we would have gotten married. I'm not saying that we still couldn't get married, but it's not fireworks. And I gotta have fireworks. I had fireworks with Sharon. But I don't want the other stuff that goes with it. The fireworks are wonderful. But I finally realized that, heart attack or no heart attack, I'm not as concerned about having the permanency, about having somebody around all the time. If I want to sit and read a book, and I'm single, I can do it. I don't have to talk to anybody if I don't want to. And if I want to get up and go to a ball game Saturday, I don't have to tell anybody. I want that. I thought I didn't want that, but I still want that. I'd like to have a marriage that allows me to say "I'm gonna go to a ball game, wanna come?" If I can't have that, I like what I have. I mean, I've come through this healthy, and not many people sit as well in life as I do. The money I'm making, the friendship I've received, the success I've been accorded, the friends I have, the relationships I've had with people. I've had one hell of a life. So the question really becomes "Who shall I let into that life?" If someone's gonna come into that life, it would have to be someone I'm not only crazy about, but like, respect, adore. And someone who has to like, respect, adore, and be crazy about me. Someone who wants me to go to the ball game because

"Larry'll have a good time at the ball game." To me the greatest love story ever written was O'Henry's *Gift of the Magi*. Because to me that's what love is all about. And unless you find that . . .

So after you have a heart attack, you realize that, yes, some things will change in your life, but not that dramatically. For instance, the experience did make me more self-confident in terms of work. If I had any doubt at all about my clout . . . I knew I had a lot of clout at work because I knew I was important to the networks. But after the heart attack I told them to back off when they asked me to come in before I was ready. They just weren't being considerate. You get a little cockier in dealing with that kind of thing. You don't let people push you around as much as they did. I guess I attribute that to just having a sense that life is, indeed, too short to take that kind of nonsense.

Also, I realize that I am a workaholic. That's not gonna change. Another thing I realized: This work is my life. Brings me great satisfaction. I didn't know how satisfying it was to me. I really get a plus result nightly from what I do. I get immediate positive feedback. I think I always knew I liked it. I didn't realize that it was kind of a love affair and that people play second fiddle to it. In other words, no woman would ever exceed it. That doesn't mean I don't think I could have a good relationship, but it will always be as a part of what I do. I think that understanding that now makes it possible for me to have a better relationship with a woman than I could have had before. If I met Miss Right, I would certainly get involved. But I'm not gonna jump up from the chair and run through the wall anymore. Since the heart attack I've decided I'm not gonna kill myself for anybody anymore. I'm not gonna go through motions anymore. The event changes everything. Some things it doesn't change. For the first five months you try to stay calm in stressful situations. Then, sure enough, you get caught in traffic and you find yourself banging the steering wheel—which you swore to yourself you'd never do. But despite the changes, you're still the same person.

But same person or not, you certainly turn inward for a period of time, examining yourself, your past, and your relationships. I found that I began to think quite a bit about my boyhood in Brooklyn, the death of my father, and the effect that had on me.

 But same person or not, you certainly turn inward for a period of time, examining yourself, your past, and your relationships.

I grew up in the East New York and Bensonhurst areas of Brooklyn. My father owned a little bar and grill on Howard Avenue in East New York. But when the war started he sold it and went to work in a defense plant. He was very patriotic. He died of a heart attack a little before D day. He was forty-three and I was nine and a half. That's when we moved to Bensonhurst, where I grew up. I was very close to him. Dad had had a son who died of a burst appendix when he was six years old, about a year and a half before I was born. So he was very close to me because he felt like he had been given another son. His death had a great effect on me. I had been a good student. Skipped third grade. But I stopped being a good student. Stopped caring about a lot of things. As far as I know, I didn't go to his funeral. You know, a psychiatrist told me once that nine to ten is generally thought to be about the age at which a child understands mortality—that his grandparents are gonna die, and his parents are gonna die, and someday he's gonna die. It's the age that James Agee chose for the hero of *A Death in the Family*— which was turned into the play *Dark at the Top of the Stairs*. Death as viewed by a ten-year-old. I've also noticed that at nine years old a child gives no thought to walking on the top of a fence, but at ten years old he knows that he's gonna get hurt. I was right around that age. Psychologists I've talked to think that I took my father's death as his deserting me.

My heart attack made me reassess all of that, but of course it was too late to do anything about it. Death is a very funny thing. There have been a lot of people who take death as a leaving. "If he loved me, he would have taken better care of himself." Just like I had taken good care of myself, right? But I definitely think that I took my father's death as him leaving me. Anyway, after his death, everything changed. We moved from East New York to Bensonhurst. We were on welfare for a year— New York City bought me my first pair of glasses. About nine months after the heart attack I went back to the old neighborhood with a film crew from the CBS program *West 57th Street* for a segment they were doing on me. And it was very strange. It was an incredibly nostalgic kind of day. It's very hard to verbalize. I think the insights I got after the heart attack, both in regard to my father and to myself, had to do with mortality. I really think I had thought I was immortal. The shocking realization that I was close to dying must have been a brutal awakening to me, since I'm convinced it led to my giving up cigarettes with no desire to go back to them. It would have to have been something like that to get me to stop.

The funny thing is that while I realized that cigarettes played a large part in my being where I was, I never "blamed" them. I don't blame myself. I never blamed the object. I never felt the tobacco company snowed me. No, this was all subconscious. It had to do with saying, "No, I don't wanna die." But now I knew that someday I was gonna die. And I realized other things—like I wanted closer relationships with the people in my life: my brother, my daughter, my son. It was all tied in with my attempting to go back to the ex-wife and all those kinds of things. All that played a great part in a reaction that the doctors tell me is not uncommon among heart attack victims. But as time passes a lot of that fixation with mortality fades. You realize that you're gonna die, but not for a while. And the things you thought were important to you at the time of the heart attack that hadn't been before? You probably once again feel they really weren't all that important. You were just grabbing for something. For example, there was a time when I was dating Sharon, about three months after the heart attack, when if she had said, "Let's go off together to Canada and we'll start a whole new life," I might have gone. That's how much weight I was giving it. Now, I wouldn't do that in a million years. They told me at GW that after a heart attack one of two

But as time passes a lot of that fixation with mortality fades. . . . And the things you thought were important to you at the time of the heart attack that hadn't been before? You probably once again feel they really weren't all that important.

things often happens: You either reaffirm your vows if you're married, or many men leave their wives for younger women and just go and roll the dice. I understand both things.

 You either reaffirm your vows if you're married, or many men leave their wives for younger women and just go and roll the dice. I understand both things.

As you go through this period of reevaluation of your life, you find all your personal relationships affected in one way or another. And you find that people's views of their relationships with you are also affected. Sometimes deeply. For instance, this whole period has been both very difficult and a period of growth for Chaia. And it's been a period of growth for our relationship. In the first place, I think she has a thing about the fact that I didn't wake her up the morning of the heart attack. She can't understand why I called my producer instead of asking her to take me to the hospital. I thought I was doing the kind thing by not involving her initially. I wanted to spare her any fear. I was overprotective. I think that hurt her. She dismisses that when we talk about it, but I've sensed it in her general attitude ever since. Things are much better now, but during those first months she seemed to pull away from me. Of course that was during the time when I was seeing Sharon, and Chaia and Sharon never got along. And I certainly don't blame that on Chaia. So Chaia didn't like my seeing Sharon. She may have understood it but she didn't like it. She was very . . . I just sensed the whole thing rocked her. She was very close to me. You know, she came to live with me when she was fourteen. A lot of her financial dependence hangs on me, and I guess daddies never die. This daddy could have died and she was crying in the hospital and I saw her and she was embarrassed, "Daddy, I don't wanna cry." I think it hit her all at once. All of a sudden she realized that I wasn't going to be around forever. In fact, later, at the time of my surgery, she finally said as much; she said that she didn't know what she'd do if a parent died. And you know what? You never accept the death of a parent.

My mother died in 1976. She was seventy-six and it was very painful to me. She was ill, so it wasn't like I didn't know it was coming. But it's a deeply painful experience. I think, at least in part, that's because par-

ents are a uniquely sane place in your life. If you have a
normal life, it's the only truly selfless love you've ever
received. You don't have to give it back, but you've got
it. And Lee Harvey Oswald had it, just the same as John
Kennedy. Oswald's mother loved him the same way
Kennedy's mother loved *him*. It was unquestioning.
And when you lose that special love, you lose that
haven. I hadn't lived with my mother in years, but
when she died it was a place I didn't have to go. It was a
place I couldn't go to anymore. No home anymore.
Your mother's place is always safe. If you're seventy
years old and your mother's ninety, the door is always
open . . . you don't have to call. It's not open from
your child, or your wife, or your brother, so when you
lose a parent at any age it's horribly wrenching.

Except for the debacle of pursuing my ex-wife, I
think all the changes that I've made in my life as a result
of the heart attack have been very positive. I've grown
closer to Chaia—in a positive sense. I think we understand each other better now. I know she needs her
space, and she knows that if I was oversolicitous, it was
because I love her. I've grown closer to my son, Andy.
And I've certainly gotten much closer to my brother,
Marty Zeiger.

There's just absolutely no question that my heart attack, and later my bypass surgery, probably brought
Marty and me closer together than we've ever been in
our lives—five times closer even than we were as kids.

A year before the heart attack if you'd asked me
about my brother Marty, the corporate lawyer, I'd have
said, "Ya, we're brothers. People have brothers, you
know?" Not that there was any real problem between
us, but we're very different people: He's great with

money; money's always been the bane of my existence; I lead a show-business, weird-hours, helter-skelter kind of life; Marty, who's the executive vice president for a pharmaceutical company, leads a very proper, nine-to-five, dark-suit kind of life; I'm an Adlai Stevenson, Mario Cuomo, liberal Democrat; Marty's a Bill Buckley, Ronald Reagan, conservative Republican; I live in one city, he lives in another. In other words, we were brothers, but we didn't think we had much in common. For years neither of us made any real attempt to keep up regular contact—at least I know I didn't.

 But you know how some people have brothers who are their best friends? Not us. We were brothers strictly because of our genetic connection. Emotion and family bond had little to do with it. Until my illness.

At the same time, except for a couple of rough periods, there was no real animosity between us. For example, Marty has a son, Scott, who's in promotion work, sort of in show biz, and he would get into Washington and come to see me, and I am really quite fond of him. And Marty is fond of Chaia, as I am of his daughter, Elyse.

But you know how some people have brothers who

are their best friends? Not us. We were brothers strictly because of our genetic connection. Emotion and family bond had little to do with it. Until my illness. As Marty says, "Our mother was the nexus, the connection. She died in 1976. Up until that point we had some sort of connection through our mother. She was the tie binding us together. Larry was living in Miami at the time, and when I'd get to Miami to see our mother, we'd get together occasionally, for a few minutes or so. I couldn't say we were terribly close. We had some arguments over money as time went on. Then, after my mother died, we had some altercations over some things, and then we were pretty distant for a couple of years."

Then when I moved to Washington, which was closer to Cleveland, where Marty was living, we started to get a little closer. As a lawyer, Marty would get to Washington on business from time to time. We did see each other more, but to be honest about it he'd have to initiate it, I wouldn't call. But if he called and said he was gonna be in town, we'd get together for breakfast or lunch or dinner. It was closer than it had been after our mother died, but it wasn't what you'd call close. And then came the heart attack.

Marty recalls he "got a call from a woman who works for CNN in Atlanta, a friend of Larry's, who works with my daughter. There was a message to call her, and a number to call at any hour. I called and she asked if I knew that Larry had had a heart attack. I certainly did not. She gave me the details and gave me a phone number for cardiac care. I called and they said Larry King was there and had had a heart attack and he couldn't come to the phone. I didn't know what else to do. Then, about twenty minutes later, Larry called—he had gotten a phone—and he told me in a kind of husky, tired voice that he had had a heart attack, and they were about to do an angiogram. They didn't know the extent of the damage, except the pain was now gone and he was feeling better. I think this was Tuesday. I asked if I should come down right away, and he said, 'Let's see what happens in the next day or so.' I talked to him for a while and that was a touching kind of

 We both realized we were getting older, and that of the immediate family, we were all we each had.

conversation—I told him I loved him and he'd be okay."

I suppose it had something to do with stress, and something to do with our great genes, but Marty was also experiencing chest pain. On occasion the pain had started to get worse, in his upper left shoulder, chest area. Sometimes an antacid would take it away. It would come and go. Then the last weekend in June he had what everyone at first thought was the "Big Kahuna," but luckily it turned out to have been a combination of angina and a hiatal hernia.

Marty says that all during this period he kept thinking about our father. A lot. "I'd think back to June of 1943. Larry was nine and a half. I was six. The day that 'it' happened, I think it was early June, I was home with my mother and grandmother and I think Larry was at the library. The police came to the apartment house. I was downstairs. It was a warm day, late morning. They were looking for an apartment. I had a sinking feeling, the police walking into the building, it was an unusual event. And it was a walk-up, and they walked up the two flights to where we lived and the kids all followed them. And they knocked on our door. I didn't know what was going on, but I followed them into the apartment. I remember one of the policemen told my mother to sit down. My grandmother was there, and she was quite aged. And the policeman talked to my mother and then my mother got hysterical.

"I remember that very well. And you know, to this day I still get a chill when a police car comes down the street—it is coming with bad news. And then a policeman went and got Larry. In later years my mother told me that my father had complained of chest pain for a few weeks, and the doctor tested him and let him go. Maybe today, with all the tests and medication, it would have been different. . . ."

During the period of my recuperation Marty and I became closer than I think we'd ever been in our lives. He says, "I found a humanity in Larry, a caring in him that I didn't feel before. I felt that I could give that back to him if it was there in him. Through the years I had always felt pride in Larry, in his accomplishments, and it turned out that he felt the same way about me—'my brother the lawyer'—and neither of us had been able to express it before. Faced with death, we found each other. But you know, I'm almost a little envious of him now, envious that this is all behind him and it's still looming in front of me."

"Faced with death, we found each other," Marty says. "But you know, I'm almost a little envious of him now, envious that this is all behind him and it's still looming in front of me."

Isn't that a kid brother for you? Always trying to catch up.

Dr. David Blumenthal—my New York cardiologist—says that he thinks that the period of adjustment and taking stock that I went through is a fairly common phenomenon for heart attack patients—although, typically for me, I may have done it all with a bit more gusto than most. "It reminds me of an old joke," David says. "The patient goes to the doctor and the doctor examines him and says, 'Oh, you know, Mr. Jones, it's terrible! It's very serious, much worse than I thought. Starting today you're going to have to stop drinking, stop smoking, and stop chasing women.' The patient looks at the doctor and says, 'Oh my God! I didn't realize it was so serious!' 'Oh yes,' says the doctor, 'it's very serious. No more smoking, no more drinking, no more chasing women.' The patient says, 'Okay, Doctor, but if I stop drinking and I stop smoking and I stop chasing women, am I going to live longer?' The doctor looks at him and says, 'No, but it will seem that way.'

"All right, it's an old joke . . . but patients have a

fear of that. They wonder, 'I'm going to do all that stuff, I'm going to make myself miserable, and is it going to benefit me?' And that's a reasonable question. We know certain things will benefit patients and you encourage them to do as much as they feel comfortable doing."

You go through all this, you have a lot of lessons to learn. In a way, if you have a heart attack and survive, you're ahead of people who don't have a heart attack—not that I'd wish this experience on anyone! But going through this forces you to really *think* about your life as almost nothing else does. It forces you to consider what's important and what isn't. And it gives you a chance to make changes and adjustments that you might otherwise never even realize you might want to make.

8

The Pain Is Back!

SO THE SPRING BECOMES THE SUMMER AND I'M LEARN-
ing to relax. Sure, I've got heart disease, but everything
seems to be pretty much under control. I'm working
my normal schedule. I'm traveling, doing pretty much
everything I'd been doing before the heart attack except smoking. I'm also watching my diet and exercising
regularly. But the pain is gone and so is the fear. And
then it begins again.

I guess it really began in the late summer with shortness of breath: I was getting too short of breath too
quickly. I loved walking, always did. So following the
heart attack, I was a dynamo every day. I mean I
walked into Washington, I walked over the Key Bridge
from Arlington to Georgetown, and then I'd walk in the
city. And so through March, April, May, I was doing all
this wonderful walking. And then I started to get these
stress pains. I was still dating Sharon during that period,
which I don't think helped, because that created a lot of
stress for me. Of course Dr. Katz said there's no way
you can determine what emotional stress does or
doesn't do. Katz said that much of what we're told

Anyway, around late summer I'd be out walking and I'd find myself short of breath. Incredible as it may seem, my old denial and fear of surgery were so firmly entrenched that I'd write my problem off to the humidity.

about the effects of stress is based on guesswork. For example, does your heart distinguish between "bad" news and "good" news? Winning the daily double or your mother dying? You get news like that, your blood pressure is going to go way up. Doesn't matter that one's terrific and one's terrible. But does your heart distinguish? Does it "know" that one kind of news is "good" and the other's "bad"? They don't know. Obviously, bringing on added stress didn't help. But to what degree it hurt? Who knows.

Anyway, around late summer I'd be out walking and I'd find myself short of breath. Incredible as it may seem, my old denial and fear of surgery were so firmly entrenched that I'd write my problem off to the humidity—Washington's famous for it's god-awful humidity. But I'd walk a couple of blocks and I'd have to stop—shortness of breath and then shoulder pain again. The symptoms were as bad as they had been in the period before the heart attack, and to some degree they were worse. So I'd take a Nitrostat, the same pill I'd sworn I'd never have to take again after the heart attack. Soon I found myself taking a great number of them. They come in a little bottle of 100. I looked at them one day and I bet I'd taken forty in a twenty-day period. I'd look at the jar and think, "Jeez, I'm way down." I was beginning to take it routinely. Obviously, I knew something was wrong.

To begin with, of course, I did everything I *could* to deny what was going on—attributed it to the summer heat, the stress, Sharon. I was going through a lot of stuff. Finally I *knew* that it was my heart, even *I* couldn't deny that. But I could try to ignore it. I knew that I was heading for that call to go in to have a stress test and knew I was going to fail the test. In fact, I didn't think the cardiologist knew it—but I knew it. I absolutely knew I was going to have a positive stress test. And at that point I knew enough about heart disease, its treatment, and my own condition to be almost 100 percent certain that after a positive stress test, the next step would be bypass surgery—the thing that frightened me more than anything else in the world. I knew the test would be bad. I just didn't know it would be as bad as it was. But I was just having too much trouble for it not to be bad. You know, I would bet that thousands of heart patients can relate to this: They dismiss their pain as something else—it's a gallbladder attack; it's gas; anything. Because most of the time, when you stop your activity, the pain stops. It rarely comes when you're at rest. So if you can get it to go away, you can dismiss it. Certainly you know the problem is your heart: I mean, you stop exerting yourself and the pain stops. That ain't gallbladder. On the other hand, you also know, "Hey, all I gotta do is stop whatever I'm doing and the pain stops." For example, sometimes I could be making love and get the pain while just kissing, sometimes never get it. I asked David Blumenthal about that, and he said that what researchers now think is that the passages through the arteries are just changing all the time. So sometimes it's like the Santa Ana Freeway at three in the morning—wide open. Other times—rush hour on a Friday night. Who knows why it's which way when.

 For example, sometimes I could be making love and get the pain while just kissing, sometimes never get it.

By August I'm having shortness of breath and pain. I know what's coming. How could I not? I mean, even at work, people *now* tell me that during that period they thought I was a little short of breath at times. Hell, I'd just walk down the hall and be winded sometimes. And sometimes I wouldn't. Sometimes I'd carry the laundry up from the valet room and I would have to stop three times. And when I say "carry it up" that means carrying it to the elevator and from the elevator to my apartment. But then sometimes I'd carry two bundles of groceries and have no pain at all. Nothing regular about it. But I knew I was having trouble. I'm getting very anxious about this, so I call the doctor and tell him I'm having pain again and he said, "Let's have you come in September 25 for a stress test. Meanwhile, let's increase the medication dosage." As it turned out, that didn't help at all. He increased the dosage of the beta blocker I was taking—the drug that is supposed to slow the heart rate and therefore reduce the amount of oxygen the heart needs fed to it through the coronary arteries. But I was obviously past the point where my disease could be practically managed with medication.

The day of the stress test, Warren Levy, the doctor who was running it, says, "Boy, I wish every one of our patients looked as good as you do." Great for my denial. Until I stood on the treadmill. Whew! I'd only been on the thing a minute and thirty seconds. I mean, they're just having me warm up when they say, "Okay, Mr. King. That's enough." Took the EKG leads off my chest and told me to go get dressed, wait outside. And then I

 Sometimes I'd carry the laundry up from the valet room and I would have to stop three times. And when I say "carry it up" that means carrying it to the elevator and from the elevator to my apartment.

saw Dr. Katz come down. It was one of those "Great Moments in Medicine." Now here's my cardiologist, right? Going in to see the doctor who just gave me the stress test. Katz goes by and says, "I'll talk to you in a couple of minutes." Goes in and closes the door. Remember how I said that when I was having the heart attack Levy and all the doctors took one look at the EKG, turned around, and headed right for me? How I *knew* this was not going to be news I wanted to hear? Same thing right after the stress test. I knew he was gonna tell me something bad. And what he told me . . . he handled it very well. His office is across the street from the hospital, so he says, "Let's walk over to my office." And I remember that it was a lovely Washington September day, not quite summer anymore, but not quite fall either.

We're on our way across the street and he said, "Mr. King"—he always says "Mr. King"—"you had a positive stress test." I said, "What does that mean?" "It means your blockage has returned. We think it's in the same artery that caused the heart attack. We're very concerned about that. We certainly don't want to see you have another heart attack. I think you're a prime candidate for bypass surgery." I wasn't surprised, but I felt fear from that moment on. He said there was no immediate emergency. He said, "Naturally, the sooner we do this, the better, but I'm not telling you you have to do this tomorrow. But we have some concern . . ." That was the word he used, "concern." He suggested I get a second opinion, so I called David Blumenthal in New York and I said, "David, the records and test results are on the way." I didn't hear from David for five or six days. And I knew that these guys are very conscientious. I kept wondering, "Where is he? Why hasn't David called?" About a week after it was mailed off I was talking to Herbie on the phone and we both decided that no news from David was good news. We figured he looked at all my tests and records and decided that I was a borderline case—didn't really need the surgery.

The following day the phone rings, I pick it up, and a voice says, "Larry? David. I'm sorry it took so long to get back to you, but in addition to the stress test I wanted to see your catheterization that was done the day after the heart attack as well. I completely concur. You have to get this surgery done. I don't say you have to do it tomorrow, but I'm not saying doing it next summer either." So I immediately start with David— I've got every excuse imaginable: contract negotiation time is coming up with CNN; we've got offers I've got to deal with on other things. I was going through an extraordinary time in my professional life. Major dollars. A book coming out in the spring. We had the offer to do this book. I mean life was riding a freakin' high. And I didn't want to go into surgery without having any of it settled. So I called my agent, Bob Woolf—who has also had bypass surgery, by the way—and told him what David wanted to do. Then I had to decide where to do the surgery—not that I was reconciled to doing it, not by a long shot! But if I was going to do it, my initial inclination was to do it in Washington. That's where I live, where a lot of people know me. I like that hospital a great deal, I've been there. Katz said the surgeon there is very good, but David went crazy for O. Wayne Isom, chairman of the division of cardiothoracic surgery and surgeon in chief of cardiothoracic surgery at New York Hospital-Cornell University Medical Center, where David practices and teaches. David tells me, "That's who I'd have operate on my own father." So I tell him, "Set it up." At that moment I finally *knew* that I was going to have the surgery, but I don't think I every truly *accepted* it until the moment on December 1 when I woke up after surgery in the cardiac care unit of New York Hospital.

Being terrified of this impending surgery was nothing new for me: I'd been terrified of it ever since 1981, when I was first diagnosed as having heart disease. Since then, though, I'd managed to push it into the back of my mind. But it had certainly been something my doctors had been thinking about. Katz recalls seeing me in his office as an outpatient a few months after the heart attack. Now he tells me that he knew back then that I was going to need the surgery. In fact, he says, over the months to come he was looking for the first excuse he could use to convince me in a rational way that I needed it. Apparently there are a fair number of patients like me who really need to be hurting in order to overcome the fear and denial and face the risk of surgery. And when he first saw me in his office after my discharge from the hospital, I was feeling terrific: I'd had a heart attack, survived, lost weight, improved my overall health, and I wasn't feeling any pain. At that point God himself couldn't have convinced me that I needed surgery. But as I described my angina pattern to Katz, telling him what had been hurting and when, he realized that I had been having a lot more angina before the heart attack than either I or the doctors had recognized. So after I explained to him what it was, prior to the heart attack, that would bring on the pain, how long it would last, where it would strike, all those sorts of things—what was "normal" for me—he said, "Okay, this is your angina, this is what I want you to report to me about. I'm calling this angina—whatever you want to call it. Fine with me if you don't want to call it angina, but I want you to let me know when you experience this whatever-it-is." And that's what I started to do. And then it became pretty obvious that, even in the early summer, there was something going on. My denial was still at work.

They gave me a stress test then, and it was really abnormal—which Katz says came as no surprise to him. But he didn't push the surgery issue with me then because he felt I'd still be too hard to convince. Katz says

> **I'd had a heart attack, survived, lost weight, improved my overall health, and I wasn't feeling any pain. At that point God himself couldn't have convinced me that I needed surgery.**

that he knew, just as I did, that I'd fail that September stress test. "I knew he would have pain and I wanted it to be a confirmation for him and myself, but even more so for him. I wanted to be able to say, 'Here you are, you're on a lot of medications. This is no way to live. Not only are we talking about the threat of having another heart attack and its affecting your longevity, but also I think this is not an acceptable life-style of running around, having a lot of pressure, and having me be anxious and you be anxious about all of this.' Be it Larry King or anyone else. This is not a situation I was happy with as a physician. I didn't care who it was, I was not happy with it. Well, as I knew he would, he failed the test at a very low level. I believe it was at a lower level than his previous exercise test. I didn't need the test to make a recommendation. I felt *he* needed it a little bit. I felt it was fair to him because I wanted to really set it up —make him an 'offer he couldn't refuse' of sorts. After the test he came over to my office very anxious. He knew what he was in for. He was anxious because he knew that the jig was up. . . ."

Although I didn't want to face surgery, didn't even want to think about it, I could see that it was becoming inevitable. But what I had difficulty understanding in all this was why things had gotten worse. After all, I'd had the tPA and the angioplasty. Stopped smoking. Changed my diet. Exercised. And I was on medication to control my cholesterol and slow my heart rate. And yet the angina was back and I was being told I needed surgery. Why?

As David Blumenthal explained it, "That return of narrowing after tPA and angioplasty is probably governed by other factors. You can have that happen to you despite the fact that you've been the paragon of virtue in terms of everything else. But it can be just a mechanical issue. Remember, when you're doing the angioplasty, what do you do? You put a balloon in there and you fracture this plaque. How do you know how it's going to heal? Is fibrous tissue going to heal across it to pull it in if it did not fracture adequately? You've exposed the inside of the plaque: Does that cause a clot to form? There are issues like that. That's different from looking at the normal vessels and seeing what happens. If you said to me, 'Listen, he had an angiogram six

months ago and here is a vessel that we didn't do anything to and now six months later that vessel has nar-
rowed, despite the fact that it had not caused the heart
attack,' that would be ominous because that would say
his atherosclerosis is progressing.

"But that didn't happen here. There were no normal
vessels that had gone bad. Basically the new problem
was not caused by too many cheeseburgers and smoking two and a half packs of cigarettes a day. The old
buildup caused it. What got Larry into the bind in the
first place was cigarettes, bad eating, and genes. Then
he had things done to him and for him and, in theory,
cleaned up his act. He came back six months later and
said, 'Wait a second. My engine is a disaster, how come?'
That's not because of failure of what he was doing.
That's a technical issue related probably to mechanical
factors or something else. Genes alone can do it to you,"
Blumenthal says. "You don't know. You don't know how
he got into the original bind. It's hard to say whether 10
percent of that was cigarettes, 40 percent was cheeseburgers, and 50 percent was genetic, or what."

So no one could really tell me why I was in the fix I
was in. And if they couldn't tell me what was really
causing my problem, and why all my changes weren't
enough, how could they be so sure that surgery was
going to be the answer?

9

Facing Reality

I HAVE NEVER IN MY LIFE BEEN AS AFRAID OF ANY-
thing as I was of bypass surgery. Never. I know that
makes no sense. I understood that the three-year mortality rate for people with my particular symptoms was
40 percent—terrifyingly high! I understood that surgery could reduce that three-year death rate to 6 percent—meaning a 94 percent survival rate. I understood
all that. Didn't matter. Nothing mattered other than
the thought of having my chest "cracked" open. Nothing compared to this, the absolute greatest fear I've
ever had in my life. One thing is a fear of the unknown,
and then there is a fear of the knife. In fact, this was fear
of the known. I knew, in essence, what they were going
to do. Fear of turning the light out after the heart attack
was "What's going to happen to me? Can I die? Am I
gonna get a pain?" You get over that after a while.
That's got nowhere to go. That is like if you sit outside
somewhere, and you're afraid a mosquito will bite you,
that fear will wane in a half hour, that mosquito-bite
fear. After two, three months of not getting pain in the
middle of the night, getting up in the morning, that

initial fear of heart attack death waned. This fear of surgery never waned. Even now, in retrospect, the thought of the cutting through the chest gives me the shakes.

As I've said, even after it was made clear to me that I needed the operation, I grabbed at any excuse I could to postpone it, managed to delay it to December 1. But needless to say, postponing the inevitable was a mistake

 The longer I had to wait for the surgery, the more scared I became. If I had it to do over again, they tell me Monday morning that I need it? Monday noon I'm in surgery. Don't tell me about it, just do it!

for two reasons: The longer I had to wait for the surgery, the more scared I became. If I had it to do over again, they tell me Monday morning that I need it? Monday noon I'm in surgery. Don't tell me about it, just do it! And the second reason that delay was a mistake was that I was feeling more and more miserable. I was doing a lot of traveling, and going through airports I'd always have to stop and catch my breath—take a nitroglycerin tablet for pain.

I remember around Halloween, a month to go to surgery, I was out in L.A. Angie met me at the airport and she had to carry my bags. She saw firsthand what it is to be a heart patient. And she was saying to me, "You like this? I mean, this is okay for you? 'Please carry my bag?' Whether it's me or anyone. And you know there is a way to stop that? Forget the longevity aspect. You'd be getting longevity thrown in as a bonus! You'd be able to live your life like *you*, not some helpless guy who's always panting for air. You're insane if you don't do it.

 "Fine, then cancel it and live with pain every day and live with grief and live with running out of breath and live with the fact that I have to carry your bag out of the airport, if that makes you feel good."

This could be stopped, for what? Two weeks of discomfort?" I'd say, "You're right, Angie. I just can't get it out of my mind that they're gonna run a knife down my chest and open it and . . ." She said, "Fine, then cancel it and live with pain every day and live with grief and live with running out of breath and live with the fact that I have to carry your bag out of the airport, if that makes you feel good." She's a tough broad. But tough just when and where you need it. It would make her strong if she were going though this. It's the view she would take. Because she wouldn't have put it off like I did. In fact, she was the only one who really put it in perspective. We were having dinner on that rainy Halloween night at a Chinese restaurant in L.A. when Angie said, "Sure the surgery's a bitch, but stop complaining. You should look at December 1 as the best day of your life, not the worst, because everything's gonna be better after that. Stop with the histrionics. In fact, you should be saying you hope you make it *until* December 1." Here I am, focusing on the fear, and she's focusing on how good it's all gonna be afterwards.

You know, once I decided I was going to have the surgery, it really is pretty bizarre how I ended up in New York for it. For that matter, consider how I chose all my physicians. First, I have cardiac symptoms and get a checkup at Georgetown University Medical Center. Do I ask them for a referral? No. I call Herbie and ask *him* for the name of a cardiologist, like he should know. Does he give me the name of the top man in Chicago? No. He sends me to his *nephew* in New York. His nephew, David, sends me to a guy *he* knew from his cardiology training at Johns Hopkins, who is practicing in Baltimore. Then, when I have my heart attack, I choose Richard Katz as my Washington cardiologist. Why? Because someone told me he was the best? No. Because he was on call when I was hospitalized and he took over my care. Then, when I need a surgeon, I end up with O. Wayne Isom, not because of his reputation, but because David, Herbie's nephew, recommends him. Now, I have to stress here that I was one *lucky* guy: All of these guys *are* first-rate. Katz is one of the best cardiologists in Washington. David Blumenthal is a Cornell- and Hopkins-trained cardiologist on the staff of New York Hospital. And Wayne Isom is one of the

brightest stars in a star-filled field. But what a way to
choose doctors!

Of course, as Katz points out, the way I ended up
with my doctors probably is not much different from
the way most people choose theirs. Whether you end
up with top people or not often depends upon who you
ask for advice, he points out. It all depends who your
"Herbie" is. Does "Herbie" give you good advice? As
he says, much the same thing happens to you when you
join an HMO, or a big multispecialty group practice.
You're going to see a doctor there. You may be able to
make some choices within the group, but once you sign
up, you've committed yourself not only to that primary
physician but to the specialists who are contracted to
provide specialty services. So once you start down the
road with the initial referral, the ball just sort of gets
rolling. That's typical of how medicine works today.

There is no question in my mind that if the doctors
had been offering me any out, I would have grabbed for
it. I would have gladly taken a limitation in my activities as an alternative to surgery. But that wasn't an
option. While the need for, and benefit of, bypass surgery is still highly controversial, and while there are
those who charge that the more than 200,000 procedures done each year far exceed the number of patients
who can benefit from the surgery, there is also a large
number of patients for whom the operation is clearly
beneficial—and I fell into that group. Not only that, but
the doctors tell me that while bypass does *not* offer
increased longevity, but only increased comfort, to
most patients, there is a small subgroup of patients for
whom the surgery does offer not only a more comfortable life, but also a *longer* life—and I was in that group.

If I had been rational at the time, I would have realized that Angie was absolutely right—I was being offered a longer, normal life in exchange for a comparatively brief period of discomfort.

Katz and other cardiologists are quick to point out that there are lots of good reasons—fear isn't one of them!—*not* to have surgery. In fact, Katz goes so far as to make a rough guess that only about 25 percent of heart attack patients are candidates for bypass, while about 75 percent aren't. The majority, he feels, should be treated with medication and the kinds of life-style and diet changes that I made. For one thing, in any individual case, the potential benefits to be gained from the surgery may not outweigh the risks of the operation: The disease may have already done its damage in one area of the heart and may not be threatening any other. Then there are patients who have so much damage, and so much narrowing all over the place, that surgery is high-risk for technical reasons, and even if it can be carried off, it's not going to give them any real improvement. Then, Katz says, there are a lot of patients in a sort of gray zone, patients who have some disease that to some degree threatens *some* of the still healthy muscle. Also, there are some patients who have no angina but have abnormal stress tests. Some have normal exercise tests but have angina. One of the hardest calls, they tell me, is where you have the patient who has angina but also has a normal stress test. Then they have to decide whether to simply treat the angina or go for early surgery. And Katz says they have to make the same kinds of decisions regarding balloon angioplasty: Should they use it as a kind of delaying tactic to postpone surgery or use it as a treatment in and of itself?

Katz tells me that "if there was one narrowing that caused the heart attack and another that didn't cause an attack, we could now do the angioplasty rather than progressing right to surgery. That's being done more and more frequently, earlier and earlier, without clear-

 "The bypass doesn't last forever in everybody," David Blumenthal told me, "and if you start to take everybody who's got minor amounts of angina or even medium amounts of angina, and do operations on them when they're young, what do you do in five or ten years when they come back?"

cut indications either. We just don't know where the break-even point is, given the small complication rate of the procedure and the small complication rate of the disease for patients at that stage. Trying to determine where one becomes a clear-cut advantage for a particular type of patient is what makes this a somewhat artistic, rather than somewhat scientific, business."

In addition to deciding *whether* to recommend a bypass, the cardiologist also has to determine *when* to send the patient to the surgeon. "The bypass doesn't last forever in everybody," David Blumenthal told me, "and if you start to take everybody who's got minor amounts of angina or even medium amounts of angina, and do operations on them when they're young, what do you do in five or ten years when they come back? It's only a really good operation the first time—the second time it's a plus/minus operation, and the third time it's a crappy operation. So you really want to do it the first time when it is absolutely required and you can count on real benefit to the individual. Obviously this is the dilemma."

Wayne Isom, the surgeon who did my bypass, tells the story about getting a call from some Wall Street hotshot in his early thirties whose father had died of a heart attack. The young guy traveled a lot, and he was scared of ending up having a heart attack in the middle of nowhere. So he wanted to know if he could arrange to have the bypass surgery right away so he wouldn't end up having it on an emergency basis sometime when he's on the road in the sticks somewhere. And there I was, having already had a heart attack, with angina, trying to duck surgery.

Blumenthal says that, while Isom takes a conservative approach to deciding when to operate, "there are a lot of guys offering the operation very quickly to a lot of people. In the short term, life is very simple for them. They're going to have more trouble in five to ten years when their patients are coming back and saying, 'Listen, I'm very unhappy now. Now I have bad angina.' The surgeon's going to look and say, 'Oh, my God! I've got to go back into that chest with all the scarring, all the good veins are gone, now what do I do?' Conversely, you say, 'Let me hold everybody off till the last minute I possibly can,' and then what do you do about the guy you lose while you're waiting? That is the dilemma: not to go too soon and use up the operation and yet not to go too late and lose people while you wait."

Blumenthal's philosophy is to establish very close relationships with his patients while trying to wait as long as possible before recommending surgery. But they have to know that it's their responsibility to call him immediately if their symptoms change, and they better be prepared for surgery. The nice, conservative "watch and wait" approach can suddenly change 180 degrees over just a few days. He has to continually drum it into patients that they can't play the denial game. He also has to deal with some surgeons with their heads screwed on straight who don't simply want to cut everybody. The temptation for the surgeon—in fact, the surgical mentality—is to want to "fix it." Which means operating. Luckily, Wayne Isom, my surgeon, doesn't think that way. When he sees someone who isn't specifically set for surgery, he'll interview the patient: "What are your symptoms like? Are your activities limited? If you're not limited, maybe you don't need to have it, except if your anatomy is such that you'll live longer by virtue of having it." I think that Blumenthal and Isom make a great team when they each talk to a patient without knowing what the other said, and it often turns out that they've told him the same thing.

So here these surgeons have people begging to hop onto the table in the OR—they literally have examples of patients in their eighties lying about their age for fear they won't get the surgery—and I'm continuing to try to think of a way out. As I said, from the time David called, I *knew* I was gonna have the surgery, but I simply couldn't accept the idea of it.

10
Checking In

SUNDAY, NOVEMBER 29, 1987. THAT DAY HAS TO GO down as the worst of my life. There is nothing I could compare it to. Much worse than my father's death when I was nine years old. It was much worse than the heart attack. Much worse. No comparison. The heart attack was pain, an emergency, take this injection in the arm. One of two things is gonna happen—you're gonna die or the pain is gonna stop. But the heart attack came, started, and ended. They gave me the tPA and I was out of pain. I stayed in the hospital eight days and never had another painful moment while I was there. But with the surgery I was scared for, what . . . two months? It was insane, because it tempered everything I ever did. In other words, I never had a totally good time from the moment they told me I needed the operation until I left the hospital after it was all over. So Sunday the twenty-ninth, the day I checked in to New York Hospital, was the absolute worst day. There was no turning back. The surgery was upon me.

Sure I'd known for about six years that sooner or later I was going to have to face this. But knowing and *know-*

ing are two totally different things. Back in 1981, '82, when I was first diagnosed with heart disease, I never worried. I smoked. I kept doing the wrong things. This just wasn't gonna happen to me. The heart attack was my awakening. And even then . . . I realize now that every one of my doctors knew I was gonna need the surgery. But I was so *terrified* of it that they didn't confront me with the reality of what was coming.

You know, I've thought about this and thought about it, and I still can't figure out what had me so scared. Oh, death. Pain. All the obvious stuff. But everybody goes through that. That's normal fear. In fact, everyone at

> **I still can't figure out what had me so scared. Oh, death. Pain. All the obvious stuff. But everybody goes through that. That's normal fear. . . . But I wasn't scared— I was terrified.**

the hospital told me there'd be something wrong with me if I wasn't scared. But I wasn't scared—I was terrified. Yet most people I'd talked to who'd been through the surgery—and I talked to a lot—gave me good reports. I only knew one person in my whole life who died during this, Vic Wertz, the baseball player. Every report I got was like the one from Bob Woolf, my agent: piece of cake; no serious pain; out of the ICU in a day;

back at work inside a week; playing full-court basketball within eight weeks; I'm feeling terrific. Duke
Snider gave me the only bad report, and it turned out I
had nothing in common with him—but I didn't know
that before the surgery. A mutual friend of ours told me
that Duke had just had the surgery and suggested that I
call him to ask about it. This was about three weeks
before I was scheduled to go under the knife. So I called
him. He was riding an exercise bicycle when I called
the house. I appreciated some of the things he said to
me. "This is a bitch," he tells me. "This is no fuckin'
joyride. It's no joyride. It's a bitch. You're glad you did it
and you breathe better, but hey, there are better things
in your life. It's a Mack-truck-hit-you kind of thing
about it. And I've had knee surgery on both knees and
that was nothing compared to this." Then he says, "I'll
tell you the absolute worst thing. When the thing comes
out of your throat—the endotracheal tube—those two
minutes are the worst pain in my life. It goes away,
right away, but God."

My fear just went from bad to worse. I mean, I figure
the big problem is what your chest feels like afterwards,
and here's Duke Snider warning me that this throat-
tube thing was the most painful experience of his life—
something I hadn't even thought about. And then I'd
talked to my friend Duke Zeibert, who also had the
surgery. He said the whole thing was easy, but his leg
hurt like hell where they removed the vein used for the
bypass. So that was something else to worry about: first
the throat, then the leg. Everybody I talked to had
some horror tidbit for me. Talk to one, he tells me the
worst thing was the catheter in the penis. Talk to another and he tells me that the definition of hell is having

those chest tubes in you. And remember I said that after the heart attack I'd talked to Al Haig about his bypass? He scared me too. Turns out that he'd given up smoking, but started again after his bypass. So on top of everything else, I'm worried about starting smoking again. At the same time, though, *everybody* I talked to said that, afterwards, you'll know that having the surgery was the best thing you could have done. So who knows why I was so scared?

Anyway. Sunday. Worst day of my life. I'd driven to New York the day before with my friend Jon Miller, the announcer for the Orioles. He took me to my brother Marty's apartment. I was going to spend Saturday night with Marty and his wife, Ellen David, the actress, and then I was going to recuperate at their place after I got out of the hospital. So Saturday night we went out for a quiet dinner—and I had to stop walking after a couple blocks, the pain was so bad. Had dinner, went back to

 Everybody I talked to said that, afterwards, you'll know that having the surgery was the best thing you could have done. So who knows why I was so scared?

the apartment, and watched a movie. Or they did anyway. I fell asleep watching. Sunday morning, I got up, had a bagel, read the papers. And then, you know, I had a nap. Middle of the morning. I think it was depression.

I had no real reason to be tired. Anyway, we were all pretty quiet that morning. As Marty says, he was almost as scared as I was—for me and for himself. And Ellen was worried for both of us. We were a hell of a cheerful crew.

So we drive down to New York Hospital at about 2:30, get there just as Bob Woolf is arriving. Much more than being my business manager, Bob is my friend, attorney, and confidant. He'll be at my bedside for most of the following week, seeing to it that everything is done to make my hospital stay as bearable as possible. Even more important, he'll be there as a constant reminder that I'm always among friends. But even the presence of family members and Bob could do nothing to change the fact that it's a typical, late November, New York day —gray, low forties. Awful. And I'm so distracted by what's coming that very little's registering. By the time I got to my room I couldn't possibly have told you what the hospital lobby looked like—and I saw later that it's a really striking place. Anyway, the way I checked in is the way everybody should enter a hospital. Anne Alexis Cote, the assistant director of the hospital and director of patient services, is there. It's "Mr. King, would you *mind* registering now? Do you *mind* answering a few questions?" The full VIP treatment. It would have been really funny if I'd been able to appreciate the humor. I realize, of course, that this isn't the way most people start their hospital stay. There was no "What's your name? Sorry, I don't see your name in my records. Who did you say your doctor is? Well, wait over there for an hour while I take my coffee break and then we'll see what we can do." None of it. This was like checking into the Waldorf. Nice work if you can get it. But you know, even with all the VIP treatment, I still felt like I was in one of those old George Raft movies, you know the scene: The condemned man is being led down the hall on death row. The chaplain's quietly reading the Scriptures. In the background an old, black con plays "Rock of Ages" on a harmonica. Just as they reach the door of the gas chamber, the warden steps forward. "Sorry, Larry," he says. "But the governor refused to grant you a stay. You gotta have the bypass!"

The room they led me to was certainly no death chamber. In fact, it was not to be believed. Corner room on the eighteenth floor. Unobstructed view to the south down the East River and Manhattan Island. View to the east of Queens and Long Island. Again, if I'd been in the mood for it, I'd have just stared out the window. Everyone else who was there with me—Bob Woolf, Marty, Ellen, Chaia, Andy, and, later, Pat Piper, my radio producer—tells me the view of the skyscrapers disappearing into that gray, rainy mist was spectacular. (Tammy Haddad, unfortunately, had to be in Los Angeles with Rona Barrett, who was doing my CNN show for me.) As was the room, with its parquet floors, wood-paneled walls, sofa, flowers from the president of the hospital. I mean, this was class. And you know what? All I remember of the room was the brown walls, the brown floors, the gray view. Beautiful as that room was, to me it has only ugly memories. I don't want to see that room. As nice as it was, I mean you couldn't have a better way to go into a hospital. But that doesn't mean it wasn't the worst experience of my life. Just a night filled with fear of death, fear of pain, fear of the unknown.

The warden steps forward. "Sorry, Larry," he says. "But the governor refused to grant you a stay. You gotta have the bypass!"

Fear of the ICU. Fear of the cardiac care unit. Fear of the tube in my throat. People tell me I was pretty nervous.

The fear aside, if they were gonna make a movie of that Sunday night I think they'd call it "The Night of the Doctors." Every time you turn around, a new doctor comes through. David Blumenthal started the parade shortly after I checked in. Stopped by to see how I was doing and to talk to me about the surgery.

 The fear aside, if they were gonna make a movie of that Sunday night I think they'd call it "The Night of the Doctors." Every time you turn around, a new doctor comes through.

I'm lying there on the bed, in my jeans, just chatting with him. "This guy's a terrific surgeon, right?" "No," says David. *"Now* I'm going to tell you he's a bum." Funny guy. Then he adds, "I have no hesitation—about

Isom or the surgery. Not a second's thought." Then I ask him what it's going to be like afterwards:

"For one week at home you're going to wish you had your money back," David tells me. "But three weeks from the day of surgery you're going to be feeling great. I have to tell you—if I were you, I wouldn't spend a whole lot of time looking at my chest afterwards. It's not a pretty sight."

"I have a little cold," I tell David, asking him, hopefully, "will that stop the surgery?" No such luck. Then David tells me that they'll know the probable extent of my surgery after they do the angiogram Monday morning and get a new, good look at my coronary arteries. He also drives home the gospel of good living once again when I ask him about exercise after the surgery. "Exercise is good for you," he tells me, "and therefore I recommend it. But the most critical things are not smoking and getting the cholesterol under control."

And then Bob Woolf adds, "All things being equal, you're going to feel better and you won't even remember you had the damn thing." If only I could have believed him.

Anyway, late afternoon and into the early evening, doctor follows doctor. The resident. The intern. The cardiology fellow. Everyone asks me for the same medical history. Listens to the same heart. Checks the pulse in my leg to make sure there are some good veins they can get for the bypass. But you go to a teaching hospital, you make a trade-off: You get some of the best doctors, who are up on all the latest advances, but you have to serve as "clinical material" for the training of the next generation of physicians.

Well, around 5:30, 6:00 P.M. there's a knock on the

door and this stranger strides—that's the only word for it—into the room. This is *no* resident. He's about my height, sandy hair, craggy face, jeans, cowboy boots, big Texas belt buckle, and white doctor's coat flapping. He's got two young guys in tow, white coats, following reverentially a few steps back. The whole thing looks like a scene right out of *St. Elsewhere.* Texas walks up to the bedside, sticks out a powerful hand, and says, in this drawl I can't believe, "Hi! I'm Wayne Isom. I'm your surgeon." "Uh-oh!" I think. "Aren't all doctors supposed to be Jewish?"

If I'm gonna be honest, I have to admit that my first impression of O. Wayne Isom, chief of cardiothoracic surgery at New York Hospital-Cornell University Medical Center, was mixed at best. I was real surprised to see this "good ol' boy" at my bedside. There's no question he had the confident, I'm-in-charge-here manner we associate with surgeons. But the cowboy boots? The jeans? Texas? Hacking open my chest? I was shocked. Shocked at his Texas attitude. Shocked at that drawl. I don't know what I expected, but I didn't expect that. You're a boy from Brooklyn, you expect a Jewish doctor, you don't expect "How y'all doin'?"

Over the course of the next week I got to talk to Wayne Isom a number of times, and in doing so I learned a great deal about surgeons in general and Isom in particular. Even in the hospital my insatiable curiosity remained intact. I found myself interviewing everybody who played a part in my care. And I certainly wanted to know as much as I could about the guy who was literally going to be holding my heart in his hands. During one of my conversations with Isom, I told him that I'd always wondered what the difference is between a good surgeon and a great surgeon.

"I don't know," Isom quipped, "I'm still working on it."

You always hear that surgeons are somehow different from other doctors, and certainly different from the rest of us. What is it that makes them different? A willingness to make decisions fast? To take risks?

"Not necessarily. First of all you have to be conscientious, you have to be obsessive/compulsive about details, you have to pay close attention to technical details, especially in cardiac surgery," Isom told me. "You can't let your mind wander while you're doing the operation. That's the major thing. I always end up using sports analogies whenever I try to tell somebody what surgery is all about, but . . . The quarterback, for instance, cannot be thinking about what he's going to be doing tomorrow, or what he's going to do this evening, or what he did yesterday. It's *right now,* and everything is *right here.* Because, as a surgeon, you will notice you may walk in with a backache, or a headache, or your feet hurt or something, and once you get into the operating room, the problem's all gone. You don't even know about it. And then when you're finished and walk out you realize, 'Oh, my back hurt.' Or 'I've got shin splints,' or 'My neck hurt,' or whatever. But you've got to have that concentration to block it and pay attention during that period of time. So there's a multiplicity of factors. You think also that surgeons have to have a lot of self-confidence, so that you feel like you can do the best job. You certainly wouldn't want somebody to operate on you whose attitude is 'Well, gosh, I'm pretty good, but there's ten other people who are a lot better than me, and I'm going try to get through this okay.' When you go through those double doors into the OR, you want somebody who thinks and feels that he can take care of whatever comes along."

Do you go into surgery because you need a specialty where you see something "broke" and you just go in and fix it?

"Yes," Isom replied. "I think surgeons in general think more concretely and less abstractly than, say, internists. Most surgeons, if they see something crooked, they want to straighten it out. You like to see results fairly quickly, and in cardiac surgery, more than anyplace else, you can. You know immediately after the

 As Wayne Isom says, "When you go through those double doors into the OR, you want somebody who thinks and feels that he can take care of whatever comes along."

patient comes off the pump that if the heart takes over and looks good, you've done it properly and it's working. You can have complications at a later date, infections, blood clots, etc., but you know fairly quickly whether you've done it right or not."

How many times, I asked, had this man who was going to "crack" my chest done the same thing to others?

"Since I started?" he drawled. "Well, I've been doing it for about fifteen years. I guess I've probably been in on or done somewhere between 7,000 and 10,000 open hearts in the last fifteen years. Of course not all of those were bypasses."

Well, at least this guy had been around the block a few times!

There was one thing in particular about Wayne Isom that really threw me. You know how you always hear about "surgeons' hands"? Got to protect those golden hands? You hear the stories about the surgeons who can tie perfect knots behind their backs, sew with either hand? Got to, right? Well, when I glanced at those golden Texas hands that were going to literally hold my heart, my heart skipped a beat: Wayne Isom's missing the top third of his left thumb. Gone. Not there.

"I was five years old and my mother was cutting the hedges in front of our house," Isom explained. "I was helping her, but she didn't know I was helping. She had said, 'Get away, don't do this, you're getting in the way.' But I went up and grabbed a handful of branches, and she didn't see me and clipped it off—the branches and my thumb. Well, if it had been maybe a half an inch more, I wouldn't have been able to do what I do. It's just luck. But since I was so young and worked on it, I can play football and basketball and all sorts of things. So it didn't affect me and I think when you have injuries like that at a young age, you learn to compensate.

"Well, when I was doing my surgical residence at Parkland, in Dallas, the OR supervisor noticed that when I'm operating I have to pull the glove up a little higher so the thumb won't hang down. She said, 'You know, the supply company makes some special gloves,

When I glanced at those golden Texas hands that were going to literally hold my heart, my heart skipped a beat: Wayne Isom's missing the top third of his left thumb. Gone. Not there.

I'll have them come in here and measure you.' And I said, 'Well do that, that's nice.' So they did. And when the order came in I was sitting in the lounge where the doctors do all their dictating and have coffee. That's where everybody sat in between cases. Well, they wheeled the supply cart into the lounge and right up front is this case of gloves that says right on it, 'Gloves for Deformed Surgeons—Dr. Wayne Isom.' I said, 'Get that out of here.' I mean, couldn't they have just said, 'Custom-made Gloves'?"

Anyone who can deal with life's bad hands like that, I figured, can do whatever he wants inside my chest.

11
Bypass Surgery

YOU KNOW, HOSPITALS ARE ABOUT THE WEIRDEST places in the world: You're in for heart surgery, they give you bacon and eggs for breakfast. You're sound asleep? They wake you up to ask if you need a sleeping pill. Monday morning, November 30, I'm fast asleep—they had given me a sleeping pill Sunday night—they wake me up to take me down for my appointment with Dr. Jeffrey Borer, who's gonna do my presurgery angiogram. First they have trouble getting the IV started—and *that's* always fun, even when they don't have problems. Then they have me get on a rolling stretcher to take me down to the cath lab. It's a weird feeling riding on a stretcher. You're watching the ceiling roll by. You think about all the doctor and hospital movies you ever saw. Whenever I watched programs like *Ben Casey* and everything, I never, ever thought that would be me on the stretcher.

Well, everybody was very nice. I'm sure they're nice to everybody, but it can't hurt to be a celebrity. You know, it's "Mr. King, good morning." The guy who came to get me on the stretcher with the doctors was very nice. The guy who assisted Dr. Borer was terrific. They told me that everything had checked out fine. My chest X ray from Sunday was good. My lungs were all right—sure better than if I hadn't quit smoking. So they wheeled me through the hall and we went down to the fourth floor. I was the first cath of the day. They were ready for me. I guess that's the advantage of being first. No waiting.

The cath lab was a real shock. They're just finishing a new, ultramodern facility, and I was one of the last patients to go through the old lab. The shape it's in now, it looks like it should be used to strip '57 Chevys, not test patients. I mean, the place was a real dump. Doesn't do much to build confidence. But I guess there's no way to avoid that when a place is in the middle of construction. And Borer—who is director of the cath labs and a chaired professor of cardiology at Cornell—and his team really seemed to know what they were doing, whether or not the lab was a mess.

I got off the stretcher myself and climbed up on the cath table. It was different from the tables I'd been on for my previous angiograms, at GW and Hopkins. The tables I was used to were completely flat, and this thing was sort of roundish, because it turns. I didn't watch the screen much, but occasionally I'd glance over. I watched the thing that was monitoring the heartbeat and . . . by that point it was kind of comforting to watch the monitor. I was used to it, from the previous caths and from being in the CCU after the heart attack. Anyway, first they give me a shot in my rear, and then a couple of locals in the thigh, where they're gonna make the incision. So they cut into the artery, and then they thread in the catheter, a very thin tube. Thread it through the artery, up through your body, to the heart. You don't feel the incision, or anything else for that matter. Just some pressure when they cut. But the artery itself doesn't have any feeling.

So, again, what they do is they make a series of dye injections through the catheter into the coronary arteries. The dye is radioactive, and they make a film of the dye going through the arteries and your heart pumping. Shows them where the blockages are, where the arteries are open, the whole thing. The first couple of shots of dye I didn't feel at all. Usually they give you a big shot first—and you feel that—but this time, I think because they needed to do some special pictures for the TIMI study because I'd had tPA, the big shot came last. Relatively few people have had tPA so far, so this is a little new to them. Borer was asking me a lot about how quickly I had gotten to the hospital at the time of the heart attack, because he seemed to be impressed at how good the muscle looked. That had to be the result of the tPA.

They go through the whole series, and then we come to that last shot of dye. It feels like . . . you know, there's no feeling like it. It's a one-of-a-kind feeling. You know the feeling of leading up to a sneeze and sneezing? That's a feeling like no other. The feeling of having to urinate, and urinating? There's no other feeling. Sexual release? No other feeling. This is another one. But of the ones I mentioned, this is the least pleasurable because you feel that you're inside, you're inside your entire body, in the bloodstream. It's 120 degrees. It's warm. It's so warm. But what it is is it's opening up all your arteries. You couldn't possibly stand it for any longer than it lasts. I guess it must be what a turkey feels

like in an oven. I'd jump out the window to get away
from it if it didn't stop. It's not pain. It's strange. And
then the way it comes off is so weird. It wears off just as
fast as it came on, and it wears off by body parts. Comes
on all at once, toes, head, arms, everything goes up 25
degrees, like from 98 to 120. But as it wears off, it wears
off from the head down. So the head gets better, down,

 **It's a one-of-a-kind feeling.
You know the feeling of
leading up to a sneeze and
sneezing? . . . The feeling of
having to urinate, and
urinating? . . . Sexual
release? . . . But of the ones I
mentioned, this is the least
pleasurable.**

down, and you feel it go right down to your toes. By
9:15 I was back in my room. The only problem is you
have to spend the next six hours lying flat on your back
with this sandbag—literally, a heavy sandbag—across
the incision, keeping pressure on the stitches and ban-
dage. That lets go, you could bleed to death. Fast.

When he looked over the films of my heart, Borer
found that there were several problems with my circulation. As he explained it, "There are two major coronary arteries, the right coronary artery and the left
coronary artery. The left coronary quickly divides into

two branches, the arterial descending, which is the bigger of the two, and the circumflex, which gives off branches that come down the back of the heart, or the sides of the heart, and that's the smaller of the two branches. The right coronary is the smallest of the three major branches. Now you had partial obstructions in all of the three major coronary systems. The risk associated with blockages depends upon their specific location and how high up they are in the artery. The higher up they are in the artery, the closer to the blood supply, and the more complete they are, the more severe the problem. The more total the occlusion, the less reserve one has to resist the various stresses that are placed on the circulatory system. So you had blockage in all three systems.

"Now in February of 1987 you suddenly developed a change in one of the blockages in the heart systems. Suddenly the circumflex became totally occluded. You had a heart attack. That sudden occlusion markedly altered the balance between the amount of oxygen that the heart muscle needed to be able to do its work and the amount it was actually getting. The entire region of muscle supplied by that circumflex artery was put in jeopardy when that vessel suddenly occluded."

Borer explained to me just how lucky I was at the time of the heart attack: There were two factors that played a big part in my survival. The first is that I'm in the 90 percent of the population born with the ability to develop what they call "collateral flow." That means that our circulatory systems are able to open new vessels that carry the blood around a blocked artery—just the way a river will change its bed when you dam it. According to Borer, current thinking is that people are born with potential channels that connect one artery with the other. Those potential channels aren't opened if somebody has no coronary disease, is in good health, what have you. Borer told me that the current theory is that the channels open in response to one of two stimuli: one is the kind of pressure imbalance you get when there's a blockage in an artery and all this blood builds up against one side of the blockage and there's a loss of pressure on the other side; the other thing that triggers collaterals to open up is an imbalance between the amount of oxygen an area of heart muscle needs and the oxygen it's getting.

Of course I already knew the second reason that I did as remarkably well as I did: I got tPA just as I was having the heart attack. To top it off, they did that balloon angioplasty within forty-eight hours of the heart attack and opened the artery even further. Then Borer tells me that most balloon procedures that are going to fail do so within six months—just about when I started to have angina again—so that may have happened to me, although they can't really be sure. But the picture Borer saw really showed a guy on a roller coaster of luck: damned lucky I made it to fifty-four without a heart attack; lucky that when I had it it was mild and I got tPA and angioplasty right away; unlucky that the symptoms were back; lucky that I was in good medical hands; and a whole lot of underlying good luck. Because Borer tells me that, assuming everything goes well in surgery, it'll be like I never had the heart attack. I'll be able to do things I haven't done in years. You know, it was amazing. I should have been jumping for joy. But I didn't react that way. Didn't even really hear the good news. I was still just focused on the horror that I thought was coming. I moved through the day in a daze.

Except . . . one thing: There was this wonderfully surreal encounter with the dietitian. She comes into my room, middle of the morning. Very attractive Filipino woman. Beautiful, in fact. She tells me that she wants to check my menu. "You're having bypass? Tomorrow? You're Dr. Isom's patient?" I tell her I am. Then she tells me that I could have lamb chops or filet mignon. I tell her I'll just have the fruit salad. "Oh," she says, "why not have the filet mignon? It's your last good

 All I heard was "It's your last meal." I must have turned white as the hospital sheet. I just stare at her, and then I say, *"Not* funny!" Bob Woolf, who was visiting with me, leans over and says, "No, Larry! She said 'last *good* meal.' " I thought I was gonna die.

meal." Of course all I heard was "It's your last meal." I must have turned white as the hospital sheet. I just stare at her, and then I say, *"Not* funny!" Bob Woolf, who was visiting with me, leans over and says, "No, Larry! She said 'last *good* meal.' " I thought I was gonna die.

Late Monday afternoon the chief of cardiothoracic anesthesiology, Dr. Pavel Illner—a tall, thin man, short white hair, very cultured Eastern European accent, looks like Alec Guinness—comes in with his resident, a short, attractive, surprisingly young-looking woman named Dr. Hillary Richardson. He introduces them both, explains that he's going to be putting me to sleep in the morning, and then asks about my medical history. Wants to know if I've ever had general anesthesia before. Do I have fainting spells? Diabetes? Liver problems? Spinal arthritis? Allergy to penicillin? Hives? Yes, when I was a kid and had my mastoidectomy. No. No. No. No. No. No.

"You should not eat or drink anything after midnight," he tells me. "You will be given a pill, a tranquilizer, between six and six-thirty tomorrow morning. They'll come for you around a quarter to seven or so. They'll take you down to the tenth floor. If you have any pain in your chest or shoulder, I must know that. We will use a local anesthesia to put in the IV, and, as you know by now, nothing in the hospital is totally painless"—Diogenes! Diogenes! I got your man! Anyway, he tells me that I'll drift off to sleep and then says that "after you are asleep, I will put a tube in your throat so I will breathe for you with a breathing machine. You should know that the chances are even that we'll have to use blood products. You will wake up the next day, Wednesday morning. You will feel something in your throat—that will be my tube. [Tell me about that goddamn tube! That was all I had been thinking about ever since Duke Snider had told me his bypass story. Worst pain of his life, that tube!] It is also likely that you are not going to remember the operating room. That is a desirable side effect of the anesthesia."

Then he tells me that I'll be kept in a holding room before they take me into the OR, and I ask why. He explains that they use that period to make sure the right patient is going into the right operating room for the right surgery. At this point I flippantly ask Hillary Richardson, "Aren't you a little young for this?"

"I'm getting older every day," she fires back.

Illner immediately jumps in: "Am I too old for this?"

"I'm scared," I tell him. It is a non sequitur, but it's what's really on my mind. The rest is all smoke screen. Illner, bless him, understands. "I will be, too, when my time comes," he says softly.

Later on, shortly before I turned in for the night, Bob Woolf was trying to reassure me: "It's not going to be anywhere near as bad as you think it is."

I tell him that years ago, when I was diagnosed as having heart disease, I started worrying about this day. When I had the heart attack, the first thing I asked after the pain subsided was, "I don't need surgery, do I?" Illner frightened me, I'm not sure why because he was very competent and very reassuring. But you know what I think it was? The fact that he said he'd be scared if he was in my position. I did *not* want to hear that. Sure, I want my doctors to be honest, but I also want guys like Illner and Isom to be God. I know that's not fashionable these days, but think about it: You're on the plane to Tokyo, have just taken off. The pilot walks back into the passenger area and says, "Ladies and gentlemen, welcome aboard the 7:19 flight to Tokyo. *If* everything goes well, we'll be in Tokyo sometime this week. I'm sure glad I'm flying this thing, not sitting back here with you. So just sit and relax, enjoy the movie, and remember, we *usually* make it." Is that what you want to hear? Hell no! You want to hear, "Listen, this flight's a piece of cake. We'll probably get there ahead of time. No problem. In fact, I'm just gonna take this beat-up copy of *Esquire* from the rack here and go back to the can and read for a while, auto pilot can get us to Tokyo, no sweat!" Well, Illner and Isom were gonna be my pilot and co-pilot. I sure didn't want *them* telling me that they'd be nervous.

Anyway, Bob tells me that he wants to "go on record as saying that next Sunday, six days from now, you're going to be sitting in your hospital room, watching the ball games, rooting for a club, mad as hell that some team is losing. And by Tuesday you'll be chomping at the bit to get out of here."

 "I'm scared," I tell him. It is a non sequitur, but it's what's really on my mind. The rest is all smoke screen. Illner, bless him, understands. "I will be, too, when my time comes," he says softly.

It was sweet of Bob to try to reassure me, but I just wasn't having any. All I could say was, "It's just never been out of my mind."

And it didn't leave my mind until they gave me my

sleeping pill around 8:30 P.M. I just spent the remaining waking hours driving poor Anne Cote, the director of patient services, crazy. I wanted to be sure that I'd have my bridge the second I woke up in the CCU, and she had promised to personally take it for me. By Monday night I had asked her about the bridge arrangements so many times, I'm sure she wanted to toss the damn thing into the East River. But she was a good sport about it and constantly reassured me that everything would be taken care of. I'm not really sure why I was so fixated on that bridge, but I guess it had to do with control—you lose it all when you're in the hospital. Control, dignity, self-image. I think hospitals intentionally set out to strip you of all three. But having my bridge, making sure I was going to have it before I had any visitors, must have been my way to maintain some control.

As I drifted off to sleep that night I had two fantasies. The first one: A doctor comes in and says, "King, we can cure everything. You don't need the surgery. You'll never have angina pain again. You'll live a long life. But you can't have sex again." I figure, I had a lot of sex in my life. I had a lot of fun. I've had a good life. I'm very sexual, but I enjoy a lot of things. Remember, that's the condition—everything else is perfect: I'm gonna live to seventy-five, no pain, do everything else I want to. Just no sex. I take the deal—and escape the surgery.

The second fantasy: I'm at my funeral. I don't know what is gonna be said, but I know who is gonna speak. Mario Cuomo will deliver the eulogy. Herbie Cohen will speak. Angie will speak. It is in Washington, and Bob Woolf has arranged the whole thing, has everybody there. It is really scary.

Next thing I know it's 6:30 the next morning and I'm

thinking, "Shit. I just got to sleep." Anne Cote was there—like she never left—along with a nurse and Diana Goldin, the hospital's director of public relations. Hell of a way to wake up. Well, Anne got all my stuff together that she was gonna hold for me. I was still worried about my bridge. Actually, it was good to have something other than the surgery to worry about, my bridge and my glasses. But even with worrying about those things, I still couldn't forget that I might not be alive in an hour. There was no way to put that out of my mind. It was terrifying. A feeling that I'll never forget. So the nurse gave me this pill, a strong Valium. Then a guy came with a stretcher. I don't remember going down the hall. Or the elevator. But I do remember the preop area. I'm lying there on the stretcher, woman asks me, "Who are you?"

"Larry King."

"Who is your surgeon?"

"Wayne Isom."

"What kind of surgery are you having?"

"Bypass." And all the time she's checking my answers against the chart she's holding, and she checks my hospital wrist bracelet. They want to make sure you're not on the Boston shuttle if you're trying to get to Washington. After that I don't remember a thing until I woke up at about 6:00 that night.

Wayne Isom tells me that by the time I got into the OR the team was assembled and waiting to go, first case of the day. They've got three or four surgeons involved. There's the cardiac anesthesiologist—in my case Dr. Illner—who gives the anesthesia, and he has an anesthesia resident, somebody who already has his—in this case, her—M.D. and is doing training in anesthesia.

And there's what they call a circulating nurse, who isn't scrubbed; that means if there's any equipment that needs to be obtained that's outside the sterile area, or anything that needs to be done outside that area, she does it. There's at least one scrub nurse—a nurse who's scrubbed to the elbows and wears a sterile gown, not a nurse who cleans things. She's the one you see in all the doctor shows who slaps the scalpel onto the surgeon's palm when he calls "Scalpel!" She makes sure all the instruments are ready to go at the right time—Isom tells me she's a real key player in the whole thing. If she's good, everything goes like clockwork. If she isn't, you got trouble. Then there are two pump nurses, the specially trained nurses who run the pump—the heart-lung machine—that takes over the circulation and oxygenation of the blood when the patient is on bypass and they stop the heart. A lot of places they just have one pump nurse, but Isom always has two, says it's like having a pilot and co-pilot. And they are very, very important. They're really vital. After all, that machine is what keeps you alive while the surgeons are down there working. So altogether you've got between eight and about twelve people directly involved. And they all gotta work together like a fine-tuned machine.

Isom explained to me that once Illner and his resident got me to sleep . . . Actually they have to use drugs to paralyze you so you can't move at all during the surgery; they also provide the right level of analgesia—pain blockage—and then the anesthesia, which is the "sleep." And they have to have your body systems all in perfect balance, with the right mixture of gases in the blood, the heart rate perfect. When you know all that, you can understand the old joke about the woman

They don't do everything right, you don't wake up. Or if you do, you'll wish you hadn't.

who comes into the anesthesiologist's office waving a bill. She is really steamed. "Doctor," she practically screams at him, "how *dare* you charge $500 for just putting me to sleep?" "Oh," the doctor replies calmly, "I didn't charge anything for putting you to sleep. The $500 is for waking you up." They don't do everything right, you don't wake up. Or if you do, you'll wish you hadn't. Anyway, once Illner and the resident got me to sleep, shortly after 7:00, one of the assisting surgeons started to remove two veins from my leg.

Isom told me that it takes them between twenty and forty minutes to remove the veins from the leg. I couldn't figure out how my leg was going to get enough blood if they took out the veins, but he explained that there are two sets: a deep set and, near the surface, a superficial set. You can take the superficial set, and the deep set can handle all the blood supply needs of the legs. In fact, a lot of women who have varicose veins have some of those superficial veins removed for cosmetic reasons alone.

In my case they were also going to use what's called the internal mammary artery, one of the main vessels in the chest. Like the veins in the legs, they can take it because there's another source of blood for the muscles the internal mammary supplies. Isom told me that although surgery's more complicated when they use the internal mammary—and not every surgeon knows how to do it—they've learned that, over time, you're better off if they use an artery for bypass rather than a vein, because the artery stands up better under the kind of pressure it gets subjected to. Another advantage in using the internal mammary is that it comes with a blood supply. It isn't completely removed, like the leg veins. They make a cut in it and then reconnect it below one of the coronary artery blockages. So they "plug it in" already connected to its blood supply.

Dr. Wayne Isom on Bypass Surgery

I don't open the patient's chest or get things ready. The other members of the team do that. But they don't run the heart-lung machine until I get there. I make all the decisions, interactive decisions, where to go. I think that's really where the experience comes in, in knowing where to go and how to get there. Cardiopulmonary bypass, being on the machine, is obviously not a natural state. You want to keep the patient on bypass as little time as possible. It's not a time that you can dillydally around. You want to get the job done and get off bypass. In the early years of cardiopulmonary bypass, back in the early fifties and sixties, if you started going over an hour on the heart-lung machine, you'd have more complications.

Now, with all the improvements, you'll
have patients an hour or several hours,
four, five, or six hours, and still do okay.
Certainly you don't like to go over four,
five, six hours, but the time is not a
particular factor. It is to some degree,
but you don't have the same pressure on
you now.

There's another factor also. When the
patient's initially on bypass, the heart's
beating and it's getting its blood supply,
but to do the operation you have to
clamp the aorta, which means you stop
all the blood supply to the heart. It's got
to stop. The heart can't move. So you
have to stop the heart, and you also have
to stop any bleeding that would be
coming out of a vessel, otherwise you
can't see to work on it. So we have to
stop the heart, and we call that ischemic
time, or clamp time. And in years past,
the early years, we used what's called
intermittent ischemia. We'd clamp for
about twelve to fifteen minutes and we'd
unclamp for three, four, or five minutes
to give the heart a drink, then we'd
clamp again, unclamp. Over the past few
years there's been a development called
potassium cardioplegia, which is a
technique in which we use potassium in
a low dose but high enough to stop the
heart. And we inject a solution that's
real cold, to cool the heart way down
and stop the metabolic rate so that you

> can actually go several hours without the
> heart beating if you reinject. And using
> that technique in heart transplants,
> obviously, when you carry the heart
> from one place to another, you can go as
> long as six hours sometimes. You're
> always better off though spending as
> little time as possible on the pump.

When they took me into surgery they were betting that they were going to do a quadruple bypass, sewing in veins to carry the blood around four blockages in the coronary arteries. But Isom later told me that when they got me opened and saw what the story really was, they ended up doing five bypasses—a quintuple. And . . . funny story. My last radio show before I went in for surgery, Art Buchwald was my guest. We started talking about the surgery, and on the air he tells me that his wife had emergency bypass surgery. Then he says, "Let's be honest—no one cares about your surgery. Your friends will listen to you for about three minutes. Acquaintances? Two minutes. Strangers? One . . . *unless* you have a quintuple bypass." So after the surgery I'm at a wedding and there's Art on the other side of the room. He spots me and he screams across the room, "I *knew* it! I *knew* it! I said you had to have a quintuple to get people to listen, you get a quintuple!" Funny guy.

Anyway, Isom told me that when they opened me up, they discovered that there was one area of blockage that was worse than they expected. So bad, in fact, that the strain of surgery started to cause some changes in my EKG before they even put me on the heart-lung machine. By the same token, another area turned out to be better than they thought. He explained that a lot depends on what angle the pictures have been taken at, what you really can and can't see on the films. They have a pretty good idea before you go in of what they're going to find, Isom explained, but they always have to be prepared for changes in the game plan. Sometimes they expect to do a quintuple, end up doing a quadruple or a triple. Or it may turn out the other way around. They just can't give you a solid number before they start. But even doing a quintuple on me, they had me on the pump for less than an hour. Isom told me that his residents have a tendency to really be impressed when someone does something fast, you know—"Hey, did you hear that Dr. So-and-So did that quintuple in forty-nine minutes?" That kind of thing. So he always has to tell them that speed is important but not half as important as quality. The quality of the job is what it's all about. "Speed's important," he says, "but *never* underestimate quality."

I wondered how they manage to do that sewing, all those tiny stitches, in such a cramped space. Do surgeons sew with both hands, and, if they do, how do they learn that kind of dexterity? Do you have to be born with it?

Dr. Wayne Isom on Surgical Skill

You practice to become a skilled surgeon. I use an example with the residents. . . . Nobody ever played basketball in the

Garden without first practicing. They
don't do it. Larry Bird practices two
hours before everybody gets there and
two hours after everybody leaves. Some
guys can shoot with either hand, but
they have to practice long and hard.
They may have a best shot, but they
better be able to shoot with either hand.
If you're going to play in the Garden,
you gotta shoot the left-handed hook,
right-handed curve, you have to shoot
jump shots. So everybody has a better
shot, and a right-hander can shoot better
with his right hand, and you don't just
grandstand it, but if you need to, you
better be able to shoot with your left
hand—and score. There's a point in some
of the connections you make in the heart
that lend themselves better to sewing
with your left hand than with your right
and vice versa. You should be able to
sew with both. Again, it just takes
practice.

I had one resident a number of years
ago who was really technically not very
good. He was smart as he could be, but
technically he just had trouble with his
hands. I used to be fairly harsh with
him, like a coach would be, you know,
telling him "You have to work on this,
do that." And over a period of two or
three years he really got good. He's one
of the best residents I ever trained,
technically very good. And his wife told

> me later that every morning after
> breakfast, for at least thirty minutes, she
> would sit there and hold two napkins
> together while he sewed, and she
> counted the stitches while he sewed that
> suture with his left and his right hand.
> So I'm sure he did that for years, no
> telling how many hours. To do it right,
> that's what you have to do. Someone
> asked me once if the skill is in the head
> or in the hands—I think it's both. You
> have to have both of them. You can have
> a fantastic armchair quarterback who sits
> back, says what should be done, and this
> and that, but you have to have the guy
> who's out there who can throw the
> passes too.

Meanwhile, my daughter, son, my brother and his
wife, and Bob Woolf are sitting in a waiting area going a
little nuts. They thought the whole thing was going to
take only about three, four hours, and the time drags on
and on. The surgery itself began at 8:45, and the record
indicates that it wasn't completely finished until 3:05—
a total of six hours and twenty minutes under the knife.
Anyway, around 2 P.M. Anne Cote and Dr. David Skin-
ner, the president of the hospital, walk into the waiting
room and tell the family that everything's great, I'm
coming off the pump, it was a quintuple bypass, and it's
okay for them to breathe. Of course I know none of this
until days later. Last thing I know was having them
make sure I was me, next thing I know I hear a voice
saying, "Mr. King, surgery is over. It's 6 P.M. The tube is

in your throat, as you knew it would be. We expect to take it out within the hour."

It was a very reassuring, nice voice. The voice, I remember that. And remember thinking, "This throat thing don't bother me that much. Where are the chest tubes?" I couldn't speak because of the respirator tube. I didn't realize that the chest tubes lie flat, just coming out of you. I had envisioned all the tubes as some sort of Rube Goldberg apparatus that runs above, around, and below you: you know, the catheter in the penis would be attached to the wall somewhere; the chest tubes would be sticking out of you like some oil well, pumping God-knows-what to some place over the bed—that kind of thing. I remember being very aware that there was no bed next to me and I was the one in the corner. And then they tell me they're going to leave the throat tube in until the morning. You know, all the awful fears I had going into this thing—the throat tube, what it would be like to see the chest tubes—none of them came true. I mean, I couldn't see the chest tubes. I never felt the catheter in my penis. I was too doped up to notice the tube in the throat. I thought it would make me gag, thought it would be like a doctor depressing your tongue. But it wasn't. So then they weighed me. The weirdest experience in your life. They put you in a thing like a hammock. They have to weigh you for fluids and . . . so they get you off the bed onto a hammock that's a scale. I felt like a piece of meat. After that, this is seven, eight o'clock at night, I asked for a pencil. I wanted to know why they were leaving the throat tube in. I write, "Why?" They tell me they want to build up my lungs. It's too soon for me to breathe, nothing to worry about. They say it won't make any difference anyway, because I'm gonna be asleep most of the time.

And that was true, because the next thing I remember is the morning. That was frightful, Wednesday morning. That's when I saw the blood transfusion. First thing I saw. I looked up and saw blood flowing into the

 I looked up and saw blood flowing into the IV. I thought, "Holy shit! An emergency. I'm bleeding to death." I *totally* forgot that Illner had told me I'd probably need blood.

IV. I thought, "Holy shit! An emergency. I'm bleeding to death." I *totally* forgot that Illner had told me I'd probably need blood. So I'm gesturing, Pencil! Pencil! Pencil! And they hand me one and I write, "What's going on?" And they say, "You're just receiving a transfusion." Bunch of nurses there. And I remember writing, "Why're you lying to me?" And they say, "This is routine. And we'll have that thing out in an hour. This is the second blood transfusion you've gotten. If you are concerned about AIDS, the odds are about one in about 250,000"—of course now they say the odds may be closer to one in 40,000. And they say, "Hepatitis is one in 300,000." And I remember trying to write, "I'm not concerned about AIDS." I was gonna write a speech. AIDS, hell, I thought I was dying then and there. I

wasn't worrying about my chances of maybe develop-
ing AIDS sometime in the future.

Then, even funnier . . . all my fear about the tube?
Duke Snider telling me that having it come out was the
most painful thing he'd ever experienced? Well, later
that day, Wednesday, a nurse comes up to me and says,
"Mr. King, I'm going to remove your tube now." First
thing I think: "How come they got a nurse doing this?
This is serious stuff—the surgeon should be doing this.
This is the worst part of the whole thing." And the
nurse tells me, "We're gonna breathe in, breathe out.
Breathe in, breathe out. Breathe in, breathe out. And
on the third 'breathe out' I'm gonna pull the tube out."
So I get ready. I totally tense up. Grab the handrails on
the bed so hard, my hands turn white. I mean, I'm
ready. So she goes, "Breathe in, breathe out. Breathe in,
breathe out. Breathe in, breathe out." And I'm thinking, "Okay, here we go, the worst pain of my life"—and
she says, "That's it. It's out." Didn't feel a thing. Not a
thing. It was like you took a lollipop out of your mouth.
You know how long I'd been dreading that moment?
God! And a few days later, when the chest tubes came
out, same thing. No pain. No pain when the catheter
came out of the penis. And these were all the things
that I'd been dreading. The only pain came when they
took out the two thin wires that ran through my skin to
a temporary pacemaker they had in in case they
needed it. That hurt. It's funny, too, because it's so
much smaller than the chest tubes, and the chest tubes
didn't hurt a bit when they came out.

I don't want anybody to think this was all a piece of
cake. It wasn't. I mean, they turn your chest into a
construction site, you feel it afterwards—for weeks. You

hurt. You ache. You're sore. You're sore as hell. But you're not in what I would call *pain.* Believe it or not, I've had *far* worse pain from toothaches, earaches, and headaches than I had from the surgery. But there's pain and there's pain. There's nothing to magnify pain, to turn aches into pain, like anticipation, fear of the unknown, just plain terror. Remember when you were a little kid and the bogeyman lived in your bedroom closet? Mom or Dad had to close the closet door every night or the bogeyman would slip out and get you? Scared you to go to bed at night? And then one bright, sunny afternoon you decided, "Hey, let's see what's in the closet!" Nothing there but your fuzzy bunny slippers, some clothes, and a load of pieces of broken toys. No bogeyman. From then on you didn't care if the closet door was open or closed. The bogeyman was dead. Well, the pain was like the bogeyman. Once the fear of the unknown was past, it was like the junk on the closet floor—it was there, but it sure wasn't gonna consume me.

So by late Wednesday, less than twenty-four hours after leaving the OR, the worst of the experience seems miles behind me. My throat's a little sore from the tube, but I'm talking. I'm seeing visitors—although they obviously still had me pretty doped up, because I recall very little of my time in the cardiac care unit. Can't remember specific faces. Who was there, who wasn't. It's all a blur, which, they tell me, may be just as well. By the next day, Thursday, they have me out of the cardiac care unit and into a private room—didn't even have to go to the step-down unit. They tell me that if I hadn't had a private-duty nurse, which I had, they'd have kept me in step down for a day. But because the nurse could be with me in the room at all times, they moved me straight to a regular room. And that's when the visitors started coming through.

Thursday afternoon, Bob Woolf had been visiting. He left before I had my dinner, but around 7:30 he came back again. Came into the room and said, "I have a really big surprise for you. A special surprise. Comb your hair. Get yourself pulled together." So I get all ready. Well, Bob represents a lot of sports figures. Sports

 In walks Angie Dickinson. You know, it was wonderful to see her, but I was kind of disappointed. I mean, I figured the big surprise was gonna be somebody like Joe DiMaggio!

figures visiting hospitals are very commonplace. I think it would be the kind of thing, if Larry Bird were in town, Bob would have him drop by. "Hey, Larry, come on in." So that's what I'm expecting. And Bob steps out into the hall and says, "Okay, special surprise, you can come in now." In walks Angie Dickinson. You know, it was wonderful to see her, but I was kind of disappointed. I mean, I figured the big surprise was gonna be somebody like Joe DiMaggio! And it was *only* Angie.

The next day, Friday, third day after surgery, they actually had me out of bed, walking, shuffling up and down the hallway. And that night I did live call-ins to both my CNN television show and the Mutual Radio show—just two, three minutes for each show. But I was back. That made me feel good. Keep up my contact with the audience, and help me maintain my professional identity.

Sunday. A week to the day from the worst day of my life. And I'm sitting on my bed, watching the football games, rooting for a team. Getting ticked off at one player or another. Just like Bob Woolf said I would. In fact, he and I were watching the games together. You know, it's funny. Bob was really terrific through the whole thing. Stayed around the entire week. Was there to support me, help out, take phone calls. But before the surgery I found myself getting annoyed, rather than encouraged, by all his reassurances. I know he meant well. And now that it's all over I know he was telling the truth when he talked about what it would be like and how quickly I'd bounce back. But at the time I was *so* sure it was going to be awful, I just couldn't believe him. I think that people who have been through something like this have to take a kind of middle-of-the-road view of it when they talk to people who are about to go through it: "No, it's no fun. Ya, it's gonna hurt. Ain't gonna be any fun. But it sure won't be the worst thing you've ever experienced. And you won't believe how fast you'll bounce back." Something like that.

Anyway, Monday they started me exercising, and Mario and Matilda Cuomo came by. I'd interviewed him on the show a number of years ago, and we'd become very friendly since—I even spent some weekends with them at the governor's mansion in Albany. Anyway, Matilda visited for about an hour and then he came by for an hour. We talked about New York politics, hospital care. He tells me about all the problems they have in New York regulating health care, jokes that he can get me a $6.00-, $7.00-a-day discount on the room. Then he says, "You know, in Queens they do this surgery in drugstores. You don't need to check into the hospital." Funny guy. And Phil Donahue came by. He was wonderful. Stayed a couple of hours. We talked about his show, my show. He told me I was really smart to stay with CNN and not go to one of the other networks. He said, "On CNN you can have somebody like Gephart on for an hour in prime time. We can have him on, but we have to have male strippers too."

So Wednesday morning, eight days, $23,287.60—and that *doesn't* include a single doctor's bill—after checking in for bypass surgery, I leave New York Hospital. Remember how I said that when I went into the hospital on that dreary Sunday I hadn't been aware of anything, hadn't seen anything? Well, as they took me downstairs to leave I noticed things: They have these glass inlays in the floor of the main entrance to New York Hospital. It's a very pretty place. Especially when you're leaving.

12
Singing the Postsurgery Blues

DECEMBER 9. WEDNESDAY. I'M FREE AT LAST. MY brother Marty and Bob Woolf pick me up and drive me to Marty's place on Ninety-second Street. He drops me off and heads for a meeting, and I start to think about what I'm gonna do. I mean, I'm tired still, but I'm restless. So I ask my sister-in-law, Ellen, where there's an OTB office, thinking maybe I'll place a few bets on the night's races. Well, we look in the phone book and there's an OTB down on Eighty-sixth Street. So what do we do? Walk over there. I place my bets, walk back. And I don't feel a bit of angina. Nothing. Oh, my legs are sore. Hell, they should be, but no pain in any way connected to the heart. God, that was a good feeling.

Funny thing was, though, the fear, the expectancy, the waiting for the pain to return stayed with me for several weeks after surgery. I had everything in the world to be happy for. I should have been on a total high. I mean, I licked the thing. Sure, I had aches and pains. But nothing so bad that I needed a serious painkiller for it. In fact, they gave me a big bottle of Tylenol with Codeine when I left the hospital and that bottle

Post-bypass depression is a really common phenomenon, but it's one that no one has satisfactorily explained to me.

still looks full—more than three months later. I don't think I took more than three of those things. Just took Motrin. Anyway, my life was on a roll. A few days after I got out of the hospital I spoke to Dr. Katz on the phone and he told me there's no reason I can't have twenty good years. "Stick to your diet and your exercise. Don't smoke. You're gonna live past the normal population." Six weeks earlier they weren't giving me much chance at five years. I got all this. Yet I was really blue. Down in the dumps.

Post-bypass depression is a really common phenomenon, but it's one that no one has satisfactorily explained to me. I just couldn't shake the thought of those days, of that room, of the ICU. I spoke on the phone to Albert Brooks, the filmmaker and comedian, and he said, "Larry, what you do is rush everything you do. I've read that the blues period is supposed to come about six months after surgery, but you've got to rush everything and have it now." Part of it, I suppose, is that I was having sweats, "hot flashes," that started in the hospital. Isom told me that it's pretty typical—it may have something to do with the period when you're on the bypass machine, but they're not really sure—and he said it would go away in a few days to a few weeks. He turned out to be right, of course, but it was still worrisome to me. Another thing is that, initially, I wasn't sleeping well, and there's nothing like insomnia to make you blue.

Isom told me that about 25 to 30 percent of his practice is made up of doctors and doctors' families, and since he's operated on psychiatrists over the years, he's asked them to explain the blues period so he could explain it to other patients. He found that some of them have gone through it, some of them haven't. And some say don't mention it to patients, because you mention it, then they'll be *sure* to go through it. Isom thinks that part of what causes the postsurgery blues is the fact that there's so much anxiety before surgery. (Tell *me* about it!) You go through it and you say, "Hey, this wasn't as bad as I thought it was gonna be. Sure wasn't any picnic, but it wasn't as bad as I built it up." So, initially, you go through this euphoria because you escaped what you thought were gonna be the tortures of the damned. And I sure did that. I remember Isom coming by on the first day when my tube was out and asking me how I was doing. Told him, "Fantastic!" But then, as they say, what goes up must come down . . . so as high as you go, you crash just as low. So you seesaw for maybe four, five, or six weeks.

One problem is that even though you've done well— don't have any real problems—you'll notice little things start to bother you that didn't bother you before. There's a pain here or there, this hurts, or that hurts, in some places that the surgeons didn't even touch. And you'll find yourself thinking, "Well, I'm not sure it was all worth it. I'm not sure I should have gone through with it. Maybe I jumped in too quick," and you'll have second thoughts about it, even though you've done well. That lasts up to about six weeks. The little aches and pains won't be so bad in the morning, but by afternoon they'll really bother you. Best analogy I know is, it's like walking around with a rock in your shoe. In the morning it doesn't bother you, but in the afternoon everything bothers you.

I think, too, that the whole hospital experience plays a part in getting the blues. When you have round-the-clock private nurses, and I never experienced that before, everything is there at your whim, because they're there for you. "Want some ice cream? I'll go get it for you. Want the paper? I'll go down and get it. A little juice? Right away." But I was glad to get to my brother's. There's a hospital smell, you get tired of the smell. There's certainly a hospital mentality. Also control. The gowns. The dehumanizing. It all combines to depress you. I also think that part of the depression has to stem from how bizarre this whole thing is. And our generation deals with it bizarrely. I mean, the idea that they can put you to sleep, literally saw your chest open, stop your heart, take veins and arteries from one part of your body and sew them into another is *bizarre*. After all, my generation remembers a U.S. President with polio. This is all very wild stuff. And because it seems so wild, it's somehow upsetting. I mean, the other night I was thinking about it again, sort of playing with my mind, and I thought, "Maybe while they were in there, they wanted to see what my vocal cords look like—have a little fun." I figured they'd check everything out. Look at your lungs, see if you have cancer. They know a lot of things from being in there. I wonder if they look around. The bizarreness of it never leaves you. See, you're looking at it as if it was someone else's chest. I think the thing that gives me grengles—that's an old

One problem is that even though you've done well— don't have any real problems —you'll notice little things start to bother you that didn't bother you before. There's a pain here or there, this hurts, or that hurts, in some places that the surgeons didn't even touch.

word we used to use to describe what you feel like when you hear someone run their fingernails over a blackboard or the guy run the spatula across the hamburger grill—is the thought of someone cutting the chest. The thought of cutting the legs doesn't give me grengles. It's the chest. It could make you nauseous. And the idea that they lower the body temperature and sort of put you in a state of suspended animation? If I had known that ahead, I think I would have walked out. It really makes me feel bad to think about it.

Now my daughter doesn't see it as bizarre at all. As Isom said to me, she's grown up with it. Open-heart surgery has been part of her life. So she's worried and concerned for me. But just like going to the moon doesn't thrill a five-year-old, and we still flip a little that the jet we're on takes off, thinking about having your chest cut open doesn't upset her. Worry, yes. Upset, no. But to me, it'll always be bizarre.

Another weird thing. I found that after the surgery

you go through a period where you'll find yourself crying for no apparent reason. Just burst into tears. First time it happened to me was just before I went to Florida in late December. Sharon and I had arranged to have dinner together in Washington. I wasn't driving yet so she picked me up, took me to a restaurant in downtown Washington. Well, it was an emotional dinner, talking about what was, what could have been, what would never be. But at one point, in the middle of dinner, in this public place, I started to weep. No real reason. I explained to her that, as part of the postsurgical process, people sometimes just start to weep—they

 Another weird thing. I found that after the surgery you go through a period where you'll find yourself crying for no apparent reason. Just burst into tears.

don't know why. And you know what she says to me? She tells me that I have a lot to cry about! Says my life's never been in order. . . . That's the last time I saw her. In case you're wondering if maybe the crying was my reaction to the emotion of the moment rather than something to do with the surgical process, the same thing happened to me on the plane down to Miami. Just —boom! I'm sitting there reading the airline magazine and suddenly I'm weeping. Guy in the next seat thought I'd lost my mind—until I explained it to him.

You know, speaking of weird or bizarre, hospitals are weird, bizarre places. I mentioned the fact that the food I was getting didn't seem to have anything to do with my disease. Well, even funnier. After the surgery Isom says eat anything you like for two weeks. David Blumenthal says, "No. Get on a diet. Right now." Isom says, "Build yourself up. You need protein." David says, "Isom doesn't know that you can get protein from a very healthy diet. Isom doesn't know that. He's a great surgeon, but he doesn't know diet." David just thinks it doesn't make sense to start eating badly right away. I mean, my clogged arteries may be bypassed, but I still have heart disease, always will. And I'll have to be on a good diet as long as I live. David says, "You want to go out and treat yourself to a pizza one night, sure. Have a steak, sure. Because you're certainly not going to do yourself in with one meal. You have coronary artery disease that's in total remission. In total remission you can have a steak and it won't kill you. But you can't just start eating whatever you want to."

David says that he can't agree with Isom's view that, as David interprets it, in order to heal you need a lot of protein, you need a lot of calories, so get them no matter what you eat to get them. David's view is that there are plenty of other ways to get protein besides high-cholesterol foods. He says, "You can be entirely as robust with fish, turkey, and some chicken as you can with anything else and get just as many calories and just as many amino acids, and whatever else you need. I have trouble with the idea of saying to someone, 'Okay, for two weeks you're going to eat the worst crap and in two weeks and a day that's it, you have found God, you throw away the milk shake,' to me that's a little bit counterproductive. And tougher."

Basically what David is saying is that you're gonna have to change your eating habits, so you might as well get with it. You have to learn what you can eat and what you can't. There are lots of places to get lists of food. Your doctor may have one for you, the hospital can help, the American Heart Association, and there are a number of books on the subject. But the important thing isn't getting the list, it's paying attention to it. It's real easy to say those old familiar words, "I'll have the porterhouse, rare, a side of hash browns, and why don't you give me an order of onion rings." But what you have to say instead is "I'll have the catch of the day, broiled, no butter, a side order of fresh broccoli with some lemon juice, and a tossed salad, oil and vinegar on the side." You know what you find out real fast? It tastes terrific. I used to eat almost nothing but red meat. I haven't had a bite since the heart attack and I don't miss it a bit. You eat chicken, fish, margarine instead of butter, lots of fresh vegetables—you don't feel deprived. And these days it's even easy to eat this way in restaurants—which I do a lot. Just tell the waiter what you need and, usually, you can get it, even if it's not on the menu. If you're gonna be flying, call the airline ahead and order a special meal—you ought to do that even if you don't have heart disease, the food's always better. And don't forget that there are still a lot of your favorite foods that are okay to eat—pasta, with a simple tomato sauce? Terrific. A nice chicken salad—without mayo? Wonderful. You get the idea. You just have to watch your calories, simply because you don't want to gain weight, and watch your cholesterol. Whether you can use salt is gonna depend on what your blood pressure is and who your doctor is. Some doctors tell you to stay away from salt, others say don't worry about using it in moderation. It's an issue they haven't made up their minds on, so be sure you talk to your doctor about it.

You know, as I looked back on the surgery a few weeks after it—already walking up to forty blocks in cold, windy weather, without any chest pain—I'd say, if somebody tells you to do this, do it. But I have to say, I still think it was a horrendous experience, one that I would not want to do over. It's scary. It's dehumanizing. It's downright awful. But if the doctors say do it, do it.

13

Recovery: A Chat with Dr. Blumenthal

ON THE SIXTEENTH OF DECEMBER, A WEEK AFTER leaving the hospital and fifteen days after surgery, I went to see both David Blumenthal and Wayne Isom for my final exams before leaving New York. My only real complaint for either was that I had a touch of laryn-

> ▶ **As I looked back on the surgery a few weeks after it— already walking up to forty blocks in cold, windy weather, without any chest pain—I'd say, if somebody tells you to do this, do it.**

gitis—which didn't have a thing to do with my heart or the surgery, I'd just picked up a bug.

But I did have lots of questions that I'm sure most bypass patients have. And David had lots of good advice for me. "Let me just talk about your condition in general, what you think and what you're doing. There's an ugly rumor that Isom told you to eat whatever you want," David began.

"It was an ugly rumor," I told him, "and that's what he told me. Twice. I went out and I had Chinese food. He said spoil yourself a little. If you're gonna do it, do it now. And once I had three slices of pizza. That's it. Then I had chicken and . . . rice and cashews, nuts."

"Chinese food is not automatically bad, by the way," said David. "It depends on the dishes you order. The cashews are not good, but lots of nuts are good, by the way. For example, walnuts are positively desirable."

Then David looked at the surgical tapes that remained on my chest, some of which were peeling off. "Okay, those look fine. When they curl up like that and go across the incision, it means they're holding nothing. You just pull them off."

"Isn't there a danger of infection?" I asked.

"No. The ones that are peeling can go. Leave the others because those are still holding. This one is still holding marginally," he said, checking a tape that was just beginning to peel. "By tomorrow it won't be holding and then you'll pull it off. The rest look beautiful. Leave them on. They'll loosen up. Wait till they loosen up. You don't want to rip the thing. All right, tell me your medicines." We discussed my medications, and then he asked me about my exercise.

"Okay. Now how far are you walking?"

"A lot. Except for the rain."

"How many blocks? What are you up to?"

"Twenty blocks a day," I told him.

"What's the biggest at one clip?" David asked.

"I walk from Ninety-third and Second to Seventy-sixth and Madison."

"So you walk a little over a mile, a mile and a half, just about. And how did it feel?"

"No pain at all."

"No angina?" David pressed.

"God, if I had angina . . ." I said, then I told him that I had just experienced a spasm of chest pain as we were talking.

"You're going to have twinges like that," he said, trying to reassure me. "Remember, he split you from top to bottom." *Now* he tells me. God, if I had known that they were gonna take a *saw*, split my sternum, and then put in these stainless-steel spreaders and open up my chest like a sewer crew's repair site . . . So everything from your neck down to the bottom of your rib cage, all the muscles in between, have been wrenched like nothing else could ever wrench them. No wonder you wake up hoping that someone got the license number of the truck that ran you over!

"I hurt more today than I did yesterday," I tell David. "I got a twinge today."

"It'll happen like that. It happens like that with everybody. This is just the way it is. One day you'll feel more limber and inadvertently you'll put on a little more stress or strain. It all goes away. It always gets better. Where you have the pain is unpredictable. Some people have it in the front, some in the back, some higher, some lower. The only thing you can be sure of is that you will have *some* pain. After all, your body has suffered a massive assault. You've suffered a legally sanctioned assault. You've been stabbed. And all to make you healthy. Does it hurt when you breathe or more so when you move?"

"Neither," I tell my cardiologist. "This is just a sharp pain coming and going."

"Okay, now remember what I told you about the Motrin, that when you stop taking it altogether, you may discover the pains get worse, in which case you can go back on to the Motrin," David reminded me.

"I didn't take the three Motrin today," I tell him.

"That may be why you're feeling it a little bit more. As I told you, I estimated the dosage. The idea of this tapering medication and the recuperation is that every three days should be better than the three days before on average," said David.

"That's the way it's been," I told him. "This thing I'm just experiencing now started in the last ten minutes. I've just been getting a little . . ."

"This is like the stock market, up and down. You just want to be sure you're in a bull market, not a bear market."

"You know, I've had zero pain in my legs."

"That's the funniest part, right. The two things you feared the most, your legs and the tube, and neither one caused you trouble," David pointed out.

"I haven't even elevated them. They told me to elevate them at night. I haven't," I confessed.

"Well, you're not swollen at all," he said, examining my legs. "You may discover that after a long plane ride, for example, when your legs have been down for several hours, you'll be more swollen. And the way you solve the problem is, when you have the opportunity to get your legs up, do it, and when you're someplace like a plane, walk around on the plane every hour. You take a stroll. All right, now, moving on. Any palpitations, skipped beats, or extra beats?"

I tell him I don't know what that means, and he says, "You don't feel them? You don't have them. Dizzy spells or fainting?"

"Yesterday morning I had I thought a little kind of three-minute sort of not dizzy, I had a little pain in the chest, a little discomfort. I didn't know what it was; it went away."

"Okay, your monitor looked good," he tells me. He had given me a Holter monitor, a portable EKG recorder they have that you wear for twenty-four hours while you live your normal life. Gives them a real picture of what the heart's doing during all sorts of activity, not just when you're lying in the doctor's office or walking on a treadmill.

"How's my blood pressure?" I ask David.

"Your blood pressure is a touch high, but it doesn't bother me. Motrin causes a little bit of salt retention, which can raise your blood pressure a little bit, so I'm not bothered by this. I've seen from your records that your blood pressure's always been within the normal range. At least we don't have *that* to worry about. Now, be quiet," he said, listening to my heart and lungs with his stethoscope. "Take a breath. Okay, there's still a little fluid back there. That's also allowed. And that may take some time to resolve after the surgery also. It just goes away over time. There's been an injury. A guy put a knife where it wasn't supposed to be. If fluid develops, it takes some time to go away. Okay, your cardiogram is fine and basically is unchanged from the cardiogram they took in the hospital at the very end, the day before you left the hospital. And I've listened to your heart, and it sounds fine."

I tell David that I'm planning to go to Florida in two days to stay with Bob Woolf and his wife, Ann, for two weeks, and he says that's fine. "I'm back on television on January the fourth, radio the eleventh. I'm gonna take one week of television before going back on radio. I'm reducing radio from four hours a night to three."

"That sounds good," he tells me. Then he gives me a short report on my medical condition, and a copy of the latest EKG, to take with me to Florida.

"How am I doing?" I ask, not that the question wasn't more than a little redundant at that point. Okay, this whole thing makes me nervous.

"You're doing beautifully," David told me. "This is usually the I-want-my-money-back visit. I swear. Okay, usually a week after getting home people have a lot of aches and pains. And the aches and pains for a lot of people outweigh the benefit. You know, they hate this, they hate that, 'maybe I made a mistake in doing it.' So you are way ahead, you're way ahead of the game. If you feel well at this visit, then in three weeks or four weeks you'll feel unbelievable, because this is just the tip of how you're gonna feel. So that's always nice if you feel well at this point."

"Oh, I gotta tell you, I have no problem with the legs," I remind him. "Every day they get a little less stiff."

"Okay, but do keep your legs up even though you don't think they're swollen, they really are," David warned me.

"I do those exercises you gave me in the hospital, I do

them at home. And the walking every day, I should do as much as I can?"

"Well, within limits, I don't want you to overdo it. You know, if you built up to a mile twice a day, that would be fine, something like that. There's no reason you have to go too much faster than that."

"How about my joining the full cardiac rehabilitation exercise program at GW?" I ask—the program I never got around to joining after the heart attack.

"My view is, I usually tell people to wait two months after the surgery before joining one of those. Now, you may be able to go a little bit sooner because you're doing so well so fast. But there's plenty of time. . . . Remember, things have to heal. The fibrosis has to go away. I mean, you just have to heal up in there, and so to rush into the exercise program . . . I'm sure your heart can tolerate it, except, you know, sometimes your chest wall can't tolerate it or your legs can't tolerate it. So don't push it. I don't believe that regular exercise over the next three weeks is going to keep those grafts open. I mean, no one believes that. The reason they do regular exercise is, it's good for you in general. You know, it conditions you and things like that."

"What does keep the grafts"—the five bypasses—"open? Having a good surgeon?" I ask.

"Well, yes. Technically, a competent job," said David, "and then the aspirin and then, of course, not smoking cigarettes, and in the long term, not smoking cigarettes and watching your cholesterol."

"The aspirin is big now?" I want to know. This was before the latest study came out suggesting that an aspirin every other day could greatly reduce the risk of heart attack—if it was taken under a physician's super-

vision and *in addition* to not smoking, reducing cholesterol, and all the other positive behaviors.

"Well, not now, I mean it has been. There was a well-
done study that suggests that aspirin used with another
drug keeps the grafts open. But everyone . . . most
people believe, I shouldn't say everyone . . . most
people believe aspirin alone will do the job. But you
should be on the aspirin."

"You know, I heard a story this morning that yesterday the coach at Michigan was taken to the hospital for
seven hours of open-heart emergency surgery," I tell
David. "He had bypass eleven years ago. They an-
nounced it. Three arteries were shut off. What happened? He just built the plaque back up again or
what?"

"Well, yes," David said. "There is no question, first,
that these are veins. Veins don't do as well as arteries. I
mean, veins are not built for the pressure that arteries
carry. Secondly, you don't know what he was doing.
Was he smoking? How was his cholesterol? Was it high?
Was it under control? Things like that. You know, statistically there's about a 2 to 3 percent per year risk of
having angina come back. Okay? So if you work it
through, given the sort of 10 percent immediate fall-off,
and then 2 to 3 percent per year, in ten years there's
about a fifty-fifty chance you'll have angina again. But
then it's not the same for everybody. The guy who did
everything right and is not a diabetic has a much better
chance than the person who smoked cigarettes immediately and did everything wrong."

"My chance should be pretty good?"

"Your chance, since I believe you had an excellent

surgeon, who I think does a careful job, and I think you're gonna do everything right, I believe that your chance should be as good as it is possible to be, which is not 100 percent—but you're doing everything right and there's nothing more you can do. I mean there's nothing more you can do than what you're doing."

I never give up. Here I've been through the whole thing. Everything looks great. And yet my next question was, "I was right in doing this, right? You don't have any second thoughts?"

"I told you," David said, cracking up, "it was a big mistake. Remember? Right after the operation I told you I thought I'd made a grievous error."

"How close are they to doing this all with lasers?" I wanted to know. "Will it be a nonexperimental thing in my lifetime?"

"Our lifetime? I think so."

"They'll just zero in on the artery and blow out the cholesterol?"

"Yeah, they're gonna burn it out. You look at the studies and they suggest that they're getting there. There's a risk obviously of the laser burning a hole through the vessel. My suspicion is, they'll get real sophisticated computer technology, which will be independent of the operator. The computer will figure out the angle of the vessel, the laser will set itself up via the computer to know the way the bends go and things like that. Because if you just go by what you're looking at, it seems as though people have a chance of going amiss, heading the wrong way. But a computer should be able to do it."

"And the laser will do what?"

"It will burn up the inside. It'll burn out the plaque."

"That should be good because then you won't have a vein, you'll have your original artery?" I asked.

"In theory you're always better off with an artery than a vein. Now the problem with the laser is that it induces an injury itself. I mean, obviously it's a burn. It's a burn and they scar. Now I don't know if anyone knows the answer. The other thing that people are working with is stents. It's a tiny device you put in to keep the artery open and it may ultimately be that the thing you do is use the laser to open it and then quickly put in one of these stents so it doesn't scar closed and you'll have some little piece of plastic or something."

"When can I drive?"

"You have to wait till Isom says you can drive. That's just purely the technical issue of what if you get into a crunch and your chest hits the steering column. You won't be happy if that happens. I suppose if you had an air bag in your car, you wouldn't care. It's not that you can't drive, it's just that concern about an accident."

"If my heart could speak, what would it say?"

Said David, "Your heart would say, 'I'm happy. I'm being fed. I'm getting the right amount of blood for a change.' That's what your heart would say, for sure."

"Isom did some job, right?"

"Oh, yeah. But you know, you see, for you it's easy to understand now—easier in a way than it is for me. You already know you don't have angina. Your angina was so crummy before that even to do what I consider limited things was awful. And walking, you're walking a mile and a half, but for you it's a big deal. For Isom and for me, well, we go for a mile-and-a-half walk, it seems like

"If my heart could speak, what would it say?"
Said David, "Your heart would say, 'I'm happy. I'm being fed. I'm getting the right amount of blood for a change.' That's what your heart would say, for sure."

nothing. I mean, think about how much better you are, but you don't even know what your capacity is yet, and you won't know that till a stress test, you know, tells just how much you really can do."

"How long before the stress test?"

"It's variable. I usually wait two months, personally, but Katz may say he likes to do them sooner. To me that's no big deal. I never feel pressed to rush in and do that."

"I won't have a positive stress test?"

"You should not have a positive stress test. That's correct. You should have a stress test that looks fine, you should be free of angina during the stress test. Katz will give you one in anticipation of your exercise program."

"So I'll have it in about two months, right?"

"Yeah, two months would be about . . . it could be as early as four weeks and I wouldn't have any problem with that. Personally," said David, "I wouldn't do it sooner. If he says he wants to, okay."

Remember how worried I was about having that stress test in September of 1987? How I *knew* that it would mean I'd need bypass surgery? Well, believe it or not, as David and I were talking about my having a stress test a few months after surgery, I was actually thinking, "This is one test I am gonna beat!"

14
February 24, 1988: The No-stress Stress Test

FEBRUARY 24, 1988. A YEAR TO THE DAY SINCE MY heart attack. And I'm on my way to GW Hospital for my postsurgery stress test. With all the stress tests I've had over the years, this is the first time I've headed for one feeling pretty good. I'd even done all right on some of them. But I'd be driving to Baltimore, smoking, thinking, "I hope I don't need surgery." Not this time. It's been a year since I've had a cigarette, and I don't want one. And having surgery's the farthest thing from my mind. This is the first time I'm thinking, "Great! Stress test today. I'm gonna ace it!"

I'm still living with heart disease—always will be. And I'm still living with some fear. But the fear's different now. For instance, two doctors have suggested that, at 163, I can stand to regain a few pounds. Can you believe that? Put weight on? But I'm afraid to. I have a fear of gaining weight. I think, "If I eat, what happens? I don't want to be fat again." But who would have ever thought that I'd have someone say to me, "Gain weight"?

I pull up to the front of the hospital, on Twenty-third

I have a fear of gaining weight. I think, "If I eat, what happens? I don't want to be fat again." But who would have ever thought that I'd have someone say to me, "Gain weight"?

Street, and I'm thinking, "A year ago today, I'm pulling into the emergency entrance up the block." God! If you had told me a year ago that I'd be pulling in here, happy, weighing 163, having undergone successful by-pass surgery . . . you just never think about what the next day's gonna bring.

Anyway, I actually find a legal parking spot on the street, feed the meter, and as I'm putting the coins in I glance at the car and think, "God, I've come a long way in a year." You see, about a month earlier I'd driven to the drugstore to pick up a prescription, and as I was leaving I backed into a fire hydrant—in the Lincoln Town Car that Mutual Radio gives me as part of my contract. They give me a new car every year. Anyway, I hear a crunch, but I don't even check it. I drove from there to the gas station, and the kid working the pump says, "Have you seen your car?" I say, "No," and get out to take a look. Well, the whole side is creamed, and I mean creamed. An enormous gash. Looked like a good $5,000 worth of damage. There's even a *hole* in the door. I was about to really blow my top when I thought, "Wait a minute, I just had heart surgery. What's a hole in a car door?" If this had happened before the surgery, I would have called Mutual from the gas station, driven right to the repair place. Instead, I decided then and there that I was gonna keep the car for the year and I

 I was about to really blow my top when I thought, "Wait a minute, I just had heart surgery. What's a hole in a car door?"

wasn't gonna have it fixed. Then every time something upset me, I'd look at the hole in the door and remind myself of what was really important. Well, I told the story of the door on my radio show, and the very next morning Mutual calls me and they say, "Are you nuts? Get the car in and get it fixed." And I did. But whenever I start to get upset, I think about that hole. Sure, I'm still a Type A. I still get burned up about some things. But I can put things into perspective a lot better than I could before the surgery. I *know* that some things simply aren't worth dying for.

Anyway, I leave the car and head for the second-floor room where they do the stress tests. It feels weird going in. I have to pass the hallway to the cardiac care unit, where they kept me after the heart attack. And I can't help thinking that the last time I was here I flunked the test in ninety seconds and was headed down the road to surgery. But here I am, filling out the consent forms, taking off my shirt, putting on my walking shoes, and having the ten EKG leads attached to my chest.

They have me get on the treadmill, and there's Dr. Warren Levy, the cardiology fellow who rushed down to the emergency room when I was having my heart attack. "Last time was a minute and a half," I remind Levy. "You gave it to me."

"I remember that," he tells me. He checks my blood pressure. "It's 115 over 80," he tells me. "That's terrific." Then he tells the technician sitting at this computerized panel to start the stress test, with the treadmill at a 5 percent grade and the surface moving so I'll have to walk 1.7 miles per hour. Levy tells me that every three minutes they'll increase the speed and the grade. "If at any point you start to get *any* chest discomfort, or your legs start to give out, let me know," he tells me.

One minute and fifty seconds. Levy tells me my blood pressure is 130 over 80. "I was out last time before this," I remind him. We pass the three-minute mark and they keep the speed the same but increase the incline to a 10 percent grade.

Five minutes and ten seconds. "How're you doing?" Levy asks.

"My mouth's a little dry," I tell him.

"That's common with exercise—and the air is dry in here. Don't worry about it."

Six minutes. My blood pressure is 140 over 75. The grade is increased to 12 percent and the treadmill speeds up to two and one half miles per hour. "I used to think that four miles an hour was just a nice walk," Levy said, "until I started giving these. That's a brisk walk you're doing." And I'm not even at three miles per hour.

Eight minutes and five seconds. My mouth is dry. My legs are beginning to feel it.

Eleven minutes. I'm going up a 14 percent grade at three and a half miles per hour. My blood pressure is 145 over 70. "I've never gone this fast—in all the years I've taken stress tests," I tell Levy. I can't claim I'm not feeling stressed, but my heart's fine.

"I don't want you to fall off. When you've had enough let me know and we'll slow it down. I think, if nothing else, this will be a confidence builder for you. Are you game to try to go a little faster? In thirty seconds we're going to go up to four and a half miles per hour and a 16 percent grade," Levy tells me. "It's a funny speed, because it's more than a fast walk and it's not quite a slow jog." I tell him I'm game. And I do it.

Thirteen minutes. They bring the machine back to level and slow down. My blood pressure has peaked at 157. Very quickly, as I cool down, it drops to 135 over 75.

"How do you feel?"

"I feel terrific. It's the best I've ever felt."

"You did great! You did *great!*" exclaims the doctor who 365 days earlier had literally brought me back from the brink.

"I'm not tired," I tell him. He explains to me that they measure oxygen consumption in something called METS, metabolic units. My last stress test, when I reached 2.5 METS, I had angina and abnormalities on the EKG. This time I hit 10.5 with no pain and a normal EKG. "I was smart to do the surgery?" I ask Levy rhetorically.

"You did great! You did great!" exclaims the doctor who 365 days earlier had literally brought me back from the brink.

"You were smart to do the surgery. Well, good job. That's all she wrote. You can put your shirt on and get out of here. And you can be assured that you can do anything you're physically capable of with no risk."

"What a difference a year makes," I told him. God, for the first time since 1981, when I was first diagnosed with heart disease, I was leaving a hospital with nothing but enthusiasm and good news.

I got out to the car—still had money on the meter. Whole thing had taken less than forty-five minutes. "Sure," I thought, "I still have coronary artery disease. Always will. I'll have to watch my weight. Watch my diet. Take medication to control my cholesterol. And I'll always carry my Nitrostat. Every heart patient does. They're your friends. Always there if you need them. But I know I won't need them. I know that if I continue to do my part, I'll continue to lick this." I thought about the grimness of a year earlier. The pain. The closeness of death. I thought about all the psychological changes I'd gone through, my fixation with my ex-wife—which was long past—and the new closeness I'd found with my brother and his wife, and my daughter and son. And I thought about how lucky I was that, if I had to have a heart attack, I had one so mild as to just be a warning, and I had it in an age when tPA was available to me and bypass surgery is as good as it is. And then I looked up at the hospital silhouetted against the absolutely clear blue sky and, honest to God, you know, I thought, "For the first time, it's great to be back!"

Afterword

Ironically, my brother Marty had to have a triple bypass in June 1988. He came through with flying colors and that time I was on the other side of the bed. But let me tell you, it was a strange feeling, being back in the same hospital, visiting him in that same ICU where I woke up after surgery, and spending a morning in the family waiting area, just as he did when I had my surgery. This time I was the one providing the reassurances. And I could honestly tell him, both before, and after, surgery, "What you're going through is no picnic. In fact, it's a bitch. But it sure is worth it."